ANNE DESMET
Towers and Transformations

Edited by Timothy Wilson
with contributions from Anne Desmet, Anne Stevens and David Lee

ASHMOLEAN MUSEUM, OXFORD
1998

Published for a retrospective exhibition at:

The Ashmolean Museum, Oxford
15 September – 13 December 1998

and subsequently touring in 1999 to:

The University of Wales, Aberystwyth
25 January – 19 February

Holburne Museum and Crafts Study Centre, Bath
2 March – 11 April

Peter Scott Gallery, Lancaster University
22 April – 28 May

Mercer Art Gallery, Harrogate
5 June – 4 July

Millais Gallery, Southampton Institute
9 – 31 July

Oriel 31, Newtown, Powys
7 August – 11 September

The Whitworth Art Gallery, Manchester
2 October – 28 November

*(Tour details correct at time of publication but may be
subject to change due to unforeseen circumstances)*

ISBN 1 85444 111 6

British Library Cataloguing-in-publication data
A catalogue record for this book is available from the British Library

Cover illustrations: *159. Building Blocks (details)*

Designed by Roy Willingham and set in Garamond
Printed and bound in Great Britain by Healeys Printers Ltd, Ipswich, 1998

This exhibition
is supported by:

THE
ELIZABETH
GREENSHIELDS
FOUNDATION

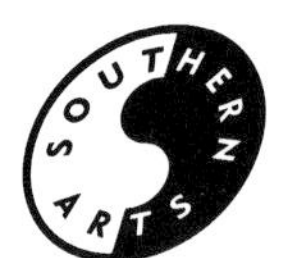

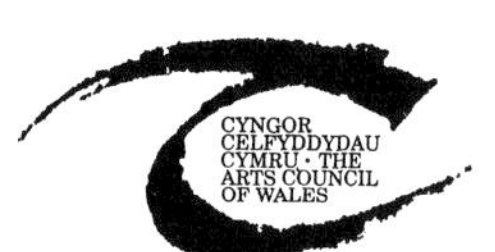

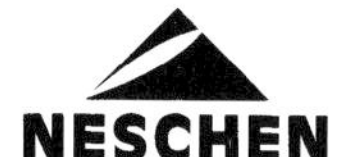

NESCHEN

8 Titan Way
off Europa Way
Lichfield
Staffs. WS14 9TT
Tel: (01543) 25 5411

filmoplast P90

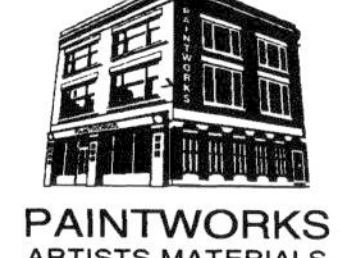

PAINTWORKS
ARTISTS MATERIALS
CONSERVATION FRAMING
0171 729 7451

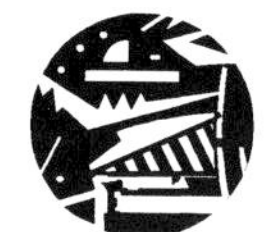

Anne Desmet's art is skilful, considered, profound, lucidly self-explanatory and intelligent, beautiful, modest in scale and requires a viewer's fixed, close-up concentration and patience. The subject of her work is concerned with studying, deciphering, translating and making a bold stab at understanding the ephemeral condition that is a human life adrift in an endlessly enduring world. It concerns how time chips at appearances and how new growth naturally, inevitably, succeeds degeneration; in short, Desmet's art addresses that relentlessness of evolution and irreversible ageing which is so bewildering to a being whose life-term is finite.

She is a wonderful artist and everyone who sees her show will know it without having to be told. It doesn't need the comments of a hack interpreter or the desperate strainings of a critic.

David Lee

Editor, *Art Review*
April 1998

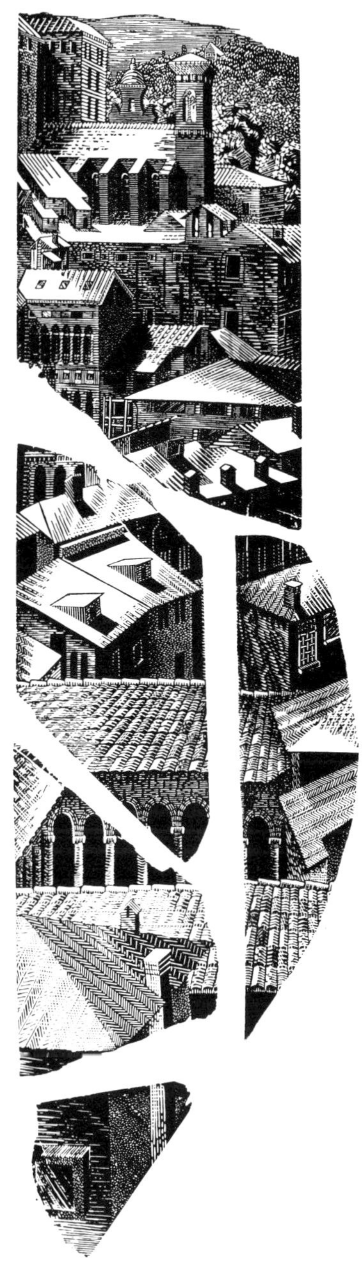

118. Bergamo (fragments)

Introduction

Anne Desmet is in her early thirties – unusually young for a retrospective exhibition and for the complete catalogue of her work to date which this book includes. But hers is a special and mature talent.

From her student days onwards, Desmet has shown ability to do something new with traditional printmaking techniques. Wood engraving in England has a strong "vernacular" tradition and the rural shadow of Thomas Bewick's well-anchored Quadrupeds still looms ponderously over the medium. A distinguished predecessor of mine once warned me about the inadvisability of "filling the Ashmolean with hedgehogs crossing the road", and though such a phrase is unjust to the talents of many gifted exponents of the medium past and present, it is always a joy to find artists, like Gertrude Hermes or Monica Poole, who radically stretch or redirect the expressive limits of wood engraving. Desmet is one such. Her wood engravings are in the meticulous tradition of Bewick in that they excel on a small scale and demand and repay close looking; but they focus on very un-Bewickian themes, especially Classical Roman architecture and its aftermaths, and metamorphosis. Her work is always immediately recognizable as hers: the fish-eye view of *Balliol College* (no. 178, illustrated on p. 5) for instance, is quite different from any other print of an Oxbridge College ever commissioned. Her transformations are frequently clever, but rarely *merely* clever: as in some of the graphics of Escher, or in good Surrealism, a balance between the amusing and the disturbing is maintained. Underlying the ingenuity and cheerful wit of Desmet's transformations is a darker sense of mutability and disintegration: the most apparently solid of her buildings are disturbingly beset by instability or prone to fall apart, even when they are not in the process of turning into something else. Much is enjoyably intangible: in *Progress/Progression?* (no. 74, illustrated on p. 22) a giraffe becomes a digger becomes a porticoed cityscape under a waning moon – or is it the other way round? It is not surprising that works made in pieces, like *Bergamo (fragments)* (no. 118, illustrated on p. 3), seem the quintessence of her work; or that collaged wood engraving has become a medium she has made her own.

The Ashmolean Print Room's holdings of twentieth century British printmaking (which have been appropriately supplemented by the deposit of the Royal Society of Painter-Printmakers) are a national resource for present and future study and enjoyment. The collection has a particular emphasis on the long-established black-and-white relief and intaglio processes; but avant-garde artists in the same technical tradition are also represented. The Museum owes the breadth of these collections (largely acquired by gift and bequest) in great part to the energy and dedication of a remarkable volunteer, Anne Stevens, whose achievement for the Museum and future students of printmaking in Britain was recognized by an MBE in 1995. Anne Desmet had left the Ruskin School of Art, and was in Rome drawing inspiration from the overlapping waves of the architecture of the Eternal City, by the time I arrived at the Ashmolean in 1990; had it not been for Anne Stevens, her work might not have come to my attention. As it is, Desmet is the only living printmaker whose work I have both admired personally and felt to fit sufficiently with the traditions of the Ashmolean Print Room to make regular purchases from her. The Ashmolean has long had a general policy of not specifically collecting or exhibiting local artists, so the fact that Anne studied at Oxford University's Ruskin School of Art is little more than a happy coincidence. Desmet's work matters on the national stage. She has shown new possibilities in her principal medium, wood engraving, and produced work that I believe future generations will continue to admire and enjoy.

I am grateful to Anne Desmet herself, for the pleasure of her portfolio-laden visits to Oxford and for taking on a good part of the organisation of the Ashmolean exhibition, its subsequent tour, and this catalogue, while I was on sabbatical leave in 1998. I am also grateful to Wendy Heppell, Ian Charlton and Simon Blake for their assistance with the exhibition's administration and publications; and to David Lee and Anne Stevens for their contributions to the catalogue. Purchases of the artist's work for the Museum collection, without which this exhibition would not have taken place, were made possible by income from the Ashmolean's Vivien Leigh Bequest Fund and from the Robin Tanner Bequest. The Ashmolean Museum and the artist wish to express gratitude to the Elizabeth Greenshields Foundation, to Southern Arts and to the Arts Council of Wales for supporting the exhibition at the Ashmolean and subsequent venues.

Timothy Wilson

Keeper of Western Art
Ashmolean Museum
May 1998

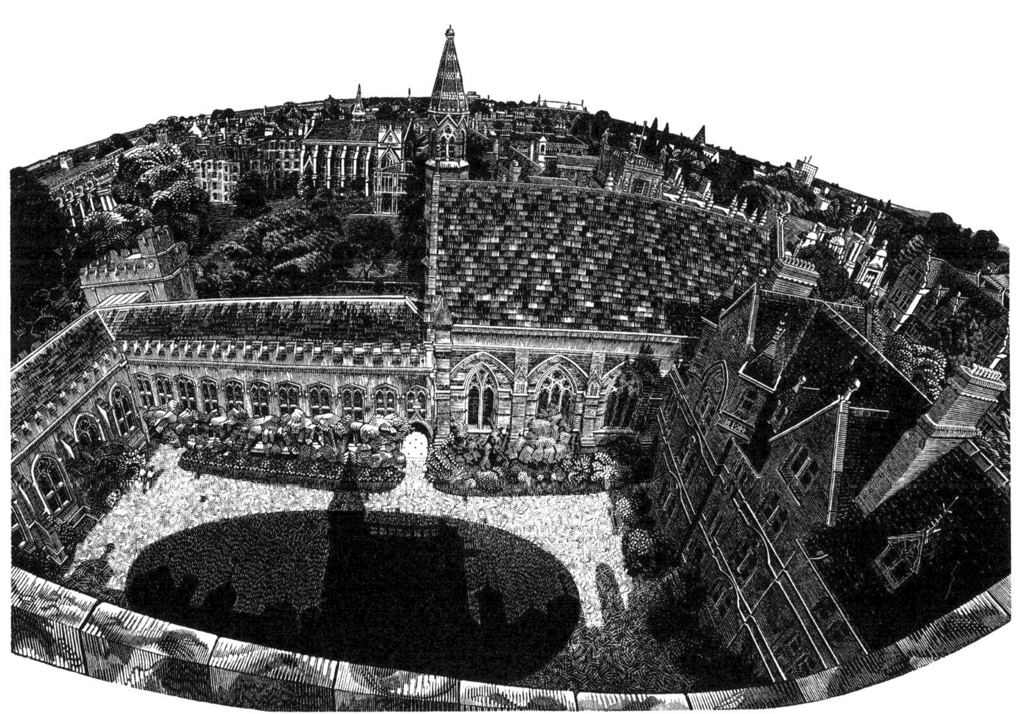

178. Balliol College, Oxford

Anne Desmet – an appreciation

Although Anne was a student at the Ruskin School in the eighties, I was unaware of her remarkable talent as a printmaker until I received an invitation to the private view of her first solo exhibition held, most appropriately, at the Ruskin School of Drawing and Fine Art in 1990. The exhibition, which included wood engravings, linocuts and collages, was clearly influenced by the year she had just spent at the British School at Rome. At that time I was a voluntary assistant in the Print Room at the Ashmolean Museum and was particularly interested in the wood engravers who flourished in the twenties and thirties of this century. On occasion this extended to the work of contemporary artists, so it was both refreshing and stimulating to see wood engravings by a young artist who seemed to be burgeoning with ideas and, at the same time, to have an innate understanding of the end grain boxwood block.

Anne came up to Oxford in 1983, academically well qualified and determined to read Fine Art. Although she had no previous art training, Jean Lodge RE, her tutor at the Ruskin School, vividly recalls her interview, recollecting the unusual and original portfolio of work she brought with her. It was Anne's good fortune to study printmaking under the expert guidance of this well known printmaker who specializes in woodcuts, etchings and mixed media. As well as providing tuition in woodcut, etching, screenprinting and stone lithography, she also introduced Anne to the end grain boxwood block, giving her every encouragement to specialize in this intractable medium. From the outset, Jean appreciated that she was an able and well organised student with the necessary determination to carry through her well thought out ideas. She received no further tuition in wood engraving as, by the time Jane Dowling visited the Ruskin School to give a brief course of instruction in the medium, Anne's way forward was determined and she remained steadfast in her ideas, sometimes mistaken by other tutors for stubbornness. Wood engraving is a demanding medium and perhaps it is worth recalling the opening sentence in Clare Leighton's introduction to her book on the subject, written in the early thirties, in which she says "Of all media, wood-engraving is the one in which there is the least to be taught and the most to be learnt".[1]

After leaving Oxford in 1986 with a BA in Fine Art, Anne embarked on a course for a Postgraduate Diploma in Advanced Studies in Printmaking at the Central School of Art and Design in London, where, largely left to her own devices, she pursued her career as a wood engraver and also produced stone lithographs under the guidance of her tutor, Bernard Cheese RE. Her other tutor was Norman Ackroyd RA RE, the eminent etcher. In 1989 she was awarded a much coveted Rome Scholarship in Printmaking and spent what she describes as "an inspirational year" in Italy. It was a revelation, as her one and only previous visit amounted to a fortnight's holiday spent in Florence and Lucca two years earlier. No doubt this must have whetted her appetite for the architectural riches she was to encounter in Rome which were to prove so inspirational. There is little doubt that she made very good use of her time, recording in her sketchbook buildings and architectural details in which the city abounds, so the theft of her sketchbook shortly before she left Rome must have been a devastating incident. However, with her usual resilience she seems to have somehow overcome this deprivation.

A glance at Anne's curriculum vitae shows, since her student days, a steady stream of awards, commissions, exhibitions – including the purchase of her work for various public collections, together with a number of teaching assignments. It was, therefore, a great pleasure to introduce her work to Timothy Wilson who had recently been appointed Keeper of Western Art at the Ashmolean Museum and, in 1992, to select with him a small group of her prints for inclusion in the collection. Since then further works have been purchased by the Ashmolean Museum.

Whilst all her prints repay close scrutiny, my preference is for her small intimate wood engravings, where she explores the passage of time in architectural terms, as in *Reconstructing the Ruins* made in 1992. It is particularly appealing and takes the form of both a limited edition print (no. 120, illustrated on p. 8) in an edition of forty and also a small book (no. 122) comprising twelve concertina-folded pages with thirteen wood engravings, limited to an edition of fifteen. Her work is succinctly summed up by James Hamilton in *Wood Engraving in Britain, c1890-1990* when he says "Architecture, and its slow passage of change, is at the root of many of the wood engravings of Anne Desmet." During the year she spent in Rome she "became absorbed by the multi-layered nature of Italian cities, one age being built upon the foundations of another. This evoked for her a strong sense of the interweaving and the passage of time, a metamorphosis which is a predominant theme in her work."[2] Similarly, her wood engraving *Forum* (no. 162), in which she collaborated with her husband Roy Willingham, is equally rewarding and rich in detail, with the ruins in the foreground and the rich roofscape of the city receding into the distance.

Her collages, which she has been making since 1990, single her out for special attention. Time consuming and ethereal, *Reflection* (no. 125, illustrated on p. 40) in an edition of one, hangs above my desk giving unending pleasure, surely the best reason for owning a work of art. A combination of wood engraving, linocut and coloured papers printed and collaged onto semi-transparent Japanese paper, the architectural images appear to float and are reflected in the lower half of the collage. It is held in place by a series of fine pins and contained within a robust box frame. Included in an exhibition of Anne's work held in 1992, at Duncan Campbell Contemporary Art, London, it took very little encouragement on Mr Campbell's part to persuade me to purchase the collage, a decision that I will not regret.

Whatever the future holds for Anne there is little doubt that, in addition to her artistic prowess and technical competence, she possesses many other qualities, such as her positive outlook on life which, coupled with her diligence and ingenuity, will undoubtedly stand her in good stead. It gives me genuine pleasure that, in addition to her exhibition at the Ashmolean Museum, her work will be seen at other venues throughout the country and will become better known to a wider and discerning public.

Anne Stevens MBE
February 1998

1   *Wood-Engraving and Woodcuts* No. 2 "How To Do It" series, Clare Leighton, The Studio Ltd, 1932.
2   *Wood Engraving and the Woodcut in Britain, c1890-1990*, James Hamilton, Barrie & Jenkins, 1994, p. 187.

Artist's reflections

At a third of a century old and having recently become a mother, this is perhaps an appropriate moment for me to look back, take stock and look forward – perhaps to move in completely new directions or to reinterpret old ideas. There is an adage that each artist only has one theme which is constantly reinvented and developed over time. That has certainly been true of my work thus far which, while dealing with a range of subject-matter, has always tended to reflect an underlying interest in ideas of time, transformation and chains of thought.

There are no artists in my immediate family, though a relative of my father was a designer/maker of stained glass in the Pre-Raphaelite style. My father, a Belgian, was an oyster farmer and hotelier, my English mother a neonatal surgeon, while my two brothers and maternal uncle are qualified engineers. I spent many months of my childhood in hospital (undergoing surgery to correct a hip defect) where I had an inordinate amount of time to live largely inside my head, so as not to become frustrated by my immobility. I recall spending hours on concentrated, observed drawings of my hands and feet and the distorted reflections of my face in light bulbs, in the bottoms of coffee mugs and so on. This experience may account for the character of my prints – with their rather still, fixed, focus points and time-consuming attention to the rendering of minute details – as well as to themes which attempt to address the slow passage of time.

At school, I was particularly interested in Latin; I think that an ongoing enthusiasm for Ovid's *Metamorphoses* combined with the impact of an exhibition of Mondrian's works, which I saw as a teenager, initiated my own ideas of metamorphosis and transmutation. This exhibition included a series of drawings and paintings in which an exquisitely rendered cherry tree transformed over a series of stages, becoming gradually more rectilinear in construction, before assuming the semblance of an abstract stained-glass window.

At Oxford, I was introduced to printmaking under the excellent tuition of Jean Lodge RE. I enjoyed the discipline involved in learning the craft skills of a variety of print methods, but felt particularly drawn to wood engraving. Its graphic clarity appealed as did the intimacy of its scale, the huge variety of marks and tones attainable in the cutting, the dramatic theatricality of creating light out of darkness (as it is the block's uncut surface which is inked), its potential for the production of sequences on multiple blocks and the attraction of irregularly-shaped blocks which often suggest their own images.

Following a year living in Italy, as a Rome Scholar in Printmaking, many of my works have been inspired by themes of architecture and landscape. My specific interest has become the multi-layered nature of (particularly Italian) cities where ancient ruins co-exist with twentieth century apartments and TV aerials, where building sites imply change and development and where edifices are often clad, completely or partially, in scaffolding; these exoskeletons help

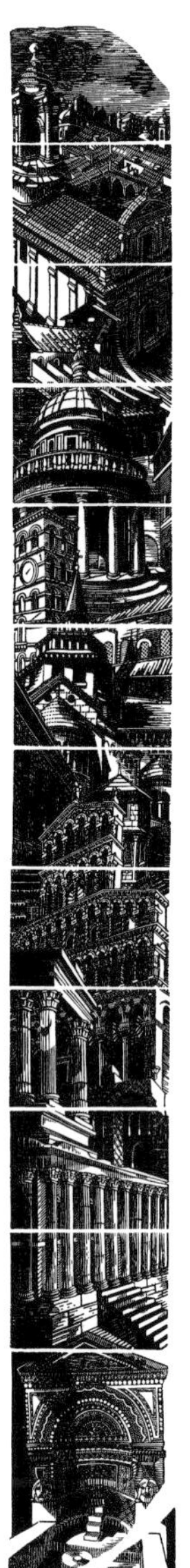

120.
Reconstructing
the Ruins

both to describe and to disguise the nature of the structures beneath but also imply a process of mutation. With such suggestions of change – indicating both the passage of time and human intervention – my intention, often, is to demonstrate how past and present influence one another; and perhaps to provoke reflection about the dangers of environmental vandalism. I aim to create a sense of the interweaving of years of history – a type of metamorphosis which is a predominant theme in my work.

I often use a sequential format to imply time, change and chains of thought – like looking at a flick-book or a series of film stills. Alternatively, I sometimes use several blocks of varying shapes and sizes on which I engrave the components of a complete image which is reassembled, like a jigsaw puzzle, in the printing. The white space between each printed block becomes an integral part of the finished print and the irregularly-shaped segments of the whole help, maybe, to convey an idea of fragile fresco fragments, of images from centuries past, seemingly timeless yet fixed in time by the presence of contemporary cars or cement mixers.

I am interested in creating, in my wood engravings and linocuts, a strong sculptural illusion of three dimensions by the use of linear perspective and a strongly contrasted range of tones. Some of my collages are, literally, in three dimensions – being low-relief paper structures. By cutting, folding, tearing, recycling and combining fragments from my prints with other paper materials, or collaging them onto gessoed and painted panels, I endeavour to create new images which are suggested by and develop the themes of my prints.

In conclusion, I would like to thank all those who have lent their support to facilitate the production of this exhibition. These include *Hans Neschen Ltd*, manufacturer of *Filmoplast P90* – a water-removable, self-adhesive, paper tape which plays an integral and invaluable part in the construction of my collages; *Duncan Campbell Contemporary Art* for ongoing support of my work; *Paintworks Ltd* for the framing of the exhibits; and my husband, Roy Willingham, for the design of this book. I am also most grateful to Dennis Andrews, David and Katharine Coleman, Barry and Val Fillingham, Professor and Mrs L G Fine, George Large, Anne Stevens, Emma Thomas, Sara Williams, Roy Willingham, and others who wish to remain anonymous for kindly loaning collages for this exhibition from their private collections. Whilst I sincerely hope that my work has yet to achieve its full potential, I am greatly indebted to Timothy Wilson for his ongoing enthusiasm for my work and for honouring me with a retrospective exhibition at the Ashmolean Museum.

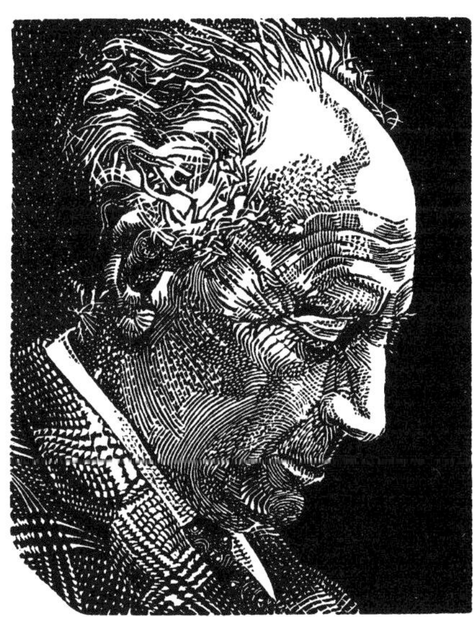

47. Louis Desmet

Anne Desmet
May 1998

Complete Catalogue of Prints and Collages (1984 - 1998)
with annotations by Anne Desmet

(* denotes works illustrated; page reference for each illustration is indicated below its catalogue number)

1 **Japanese-style Tree**

    1984   302 x 254 mm   Not editioned   Woodcut

My first print – a reduction plywood cut, printed in three colours. It was developed from a sketch made in the botanic gardens of Magdalen College, Oxford.

2 **The Belvedere Torso**

    1984   302 x 254 mm   Not editioned   Woodcut

My second print used the same technique as no. 1 and was based on a pen and wash sketch made in Oxford's Cast Gallery.

3 **Gargoyle**

    1984   168 x 152 mm   Not editioned   Etching

Worcester College (Oxford) & private collections

My first etching used hard ground and aquatint. It was based on a sketch made, as a teenager, of a gargoyle on the facade of the decaying but beautiful shell of St Luke's church in Liverpool's city centre. The church was bombed in the War and has been left in its roofless, windowless state as a memorial. I found it a poignant spot which suited my apprehensive frame of mind, prior to leaving school – after which I was to defer entry to university in order to spend months in hospital, having the last of many operations to correct a defective hip. My etching attempted to play with the structure of the sculpture – parts are stretched as if the stone has softened like chewing gum – but has been pulled taut like stretched sheets.

4 **Graffiti**

    1984   195 x 247 mm   Not editioned   Etching

An etching using hard and soft ground, the plate was bevelled in an irregular shape to suggest a slab of stone of the Temple of Poseidon. The temple stands exposed on a hilltop overlooking the sea at Sounion, Greece, and its stones bear the graffiti of generations of visitors including Lord Byron. (The image is based on a watercolour sketch.)

5 **Coloured Man**

    1984   290 x 230 mm   Edition: 6   Three-block woodcut

6 **Dryads**

    1984   102 x 76 mm   Not editioned   Wood engraving

Private collections

My first wood engraving used marks suggested by the woodcuts of Dürer. I did not know, then, that wood engraving could be used to attain a much wider, subtler vocabulary of marks than these. The subject-matter was derived from Ovid's *Metamorphoses*. The female figure was my first self-portrait and the male was based on a sketch made, while at school, of a painting of St Jerome by Andrea Alessi – in Liverpool's Walker Art Gallery.

7 **Mandrake**

    1984   102 x 76 mm   Not editioned   Wood engraving

Private collections

This print developed from a drawing, in pen and ink, produced for a poster for an Oxford students' play: *Mandragola*.

8 **War**

    1984   102 x 76 mm   Not editioned   Wood engraving

Private collections

An image based on pen drawings I made for the poster of an Oxford students' production of *Oh What a Lovely War*.

9   **Greek Fishing Boat**
    1985   200 x 125 mm   Edition: 5 A/P's   Three-block woodcut
                  Private collections
While I was at university, my family spent two summer holidays on the Greek island of Alonissos. I spent a lot of time making watercolour sketches of the island and the sea. This (and no. 10) was developed from these sketches.

10 **Alley, Alonissos**
    1985   271 x 203 mm   Edition: 10   Three-block woodcut
                  Worcester College (Oxford) & private collections

11 **Metamorphosis**
    1985   Size of each block: 82 x 76 mm   Not editioned   Seven wood engravings
                  Private collections
I have long been interested in ideas of metamorphosis. This image (produced as a sequential series of prints, a wall frieze, a flick-book and a short, animated video) was based on a coloured pencil and ballpoint pen drawing made at age seventeen.

12 **Tree with Snow**
    1985   305 x 179 mm   Edition: 10   Woodcut
                  Worcester College (Oxford) & private collections
Based on a sketch of a (now felled or toppled) leafless, snow-covered tree in the grounds of Worcester College, Oxford.

13 **Cavemen**
    1985   200 x 150 mm   Edition: 15   Wood engraving
                  Private collections
An image with an idea of transmutation – of figures turned to stone but melting back and forth from flesh to rock face. The figures were based on pencil and wash studies made in the liferoom at Ruskin School of Drawing.

14 **Self-Portrait**
    1986   172 x 231 mm   Edition: 2   Photo etching
                  Private collections
An etching developed from a photograph of me reflected in the mirror of my bedroom in my family's house in Liverpool, on the day I arrived home after a long spell in hospital, in 1983. To take the photo, I propped myself against the wash-hand basin for support, as I could not walk without crutches at that time.

15 **Anne-agrams**
    1986   470 x 419 mm   Edition: 5   Photo etching
                  Private collections

16 **Fish I**
    1986   22 x 40 mm   Edition: 20   Wood engraving

17 **Pelagos**
    1986   102 x 76 mm   Edition: 10   Wood engraving
                  Private collections

18   **Man becomes Mountain**

        1986   102 x 310 mm   Edition: 5   Wood engraving
        Private collections

Based on a study (in ballpoint pen) in the life-room at Ruskin School and a watercolour made on the Greek island of Pelagos, I connected the two images (over a metamorphosing sequence of four engravings) partly because the hunched shape of the figure seemed to reflect the curve of the hill. It also reflects an interest in Henry Moore's landscape-like sculpted figures. The final image of the sequence is also editioned on its own as no. 17.

19 *   **Sea Cycle**

(p. 13)   1986   300 x 300 mm   Edition: 2   Etching
        Ashmolean Museum & private collections

This etching was based on pencil sketches of a piece of driftwood found on the beach near my childhood home, on the Mersey coast, near Liverpool. The driftwood seemed to suggest shapes of fish and other sea creatures – perhaps like a fossilized fish skeleton at the end of a life cycle, or mouldable clay at the beginning.

20   **Fish II**

        1986   60 x 60 mm   Edition: 15   Wood engraving
        Ex Libris Museum (Moscow, Russia) & private collections

21   **Me & My Tricycle**

        1986   80 x 240 mm   Edition: 10   Wood engraving

This self-portrait depicts me undergoing a cartoon-like transformation into my tricycle. In my third year at Oxford, I learnt to ride a tricycle. I have never been able to ride a bicycle but my trike brought me an incredible sense of freedom. This portrait was intended to suggest the fun of this adult's version of a child's plaything, as well as the forgetting of oneself (and one's physical limitations) that comes with the pleasure of cycling.

22   **Anna, Sarah & Helen made Music . . .**

        1986   200 x 150 mm   Edition: 16   Wood engraving

Portraits of three students of music, superimposed into the woodgrain of a seemingly exploded wooden organ. The title is intended to imply the musicians' performing of music but also a sense of their becoming so involved in that performance that they might perhaps become a physical extension of their instrument. The "instrument" depicted was a wooden sculpture I made as a student.

23   **Icy Triton**

        1986   150 x 100 mm   Edition: 16   Wood engraving
        Private collections

An engraving of the fountain outside the Radcliffe Infirmary, Oxford, frozen in midwinter.

24   **Edinburgh Botanical Gardens**

        1986   270 x 205 mm   Edition: 6   Etching
        Private collections

This and no. 25 were derived from felt-pen sketches of the gardens and glasshouses made between bouts of busking as a singer with a jazz band at Edinburgh's Fringe Festival.

25   **Edinburgh Botanical Gardens**

        1986   265 x 198 mm   Edition: 12   Stone lithograph
        Private collections

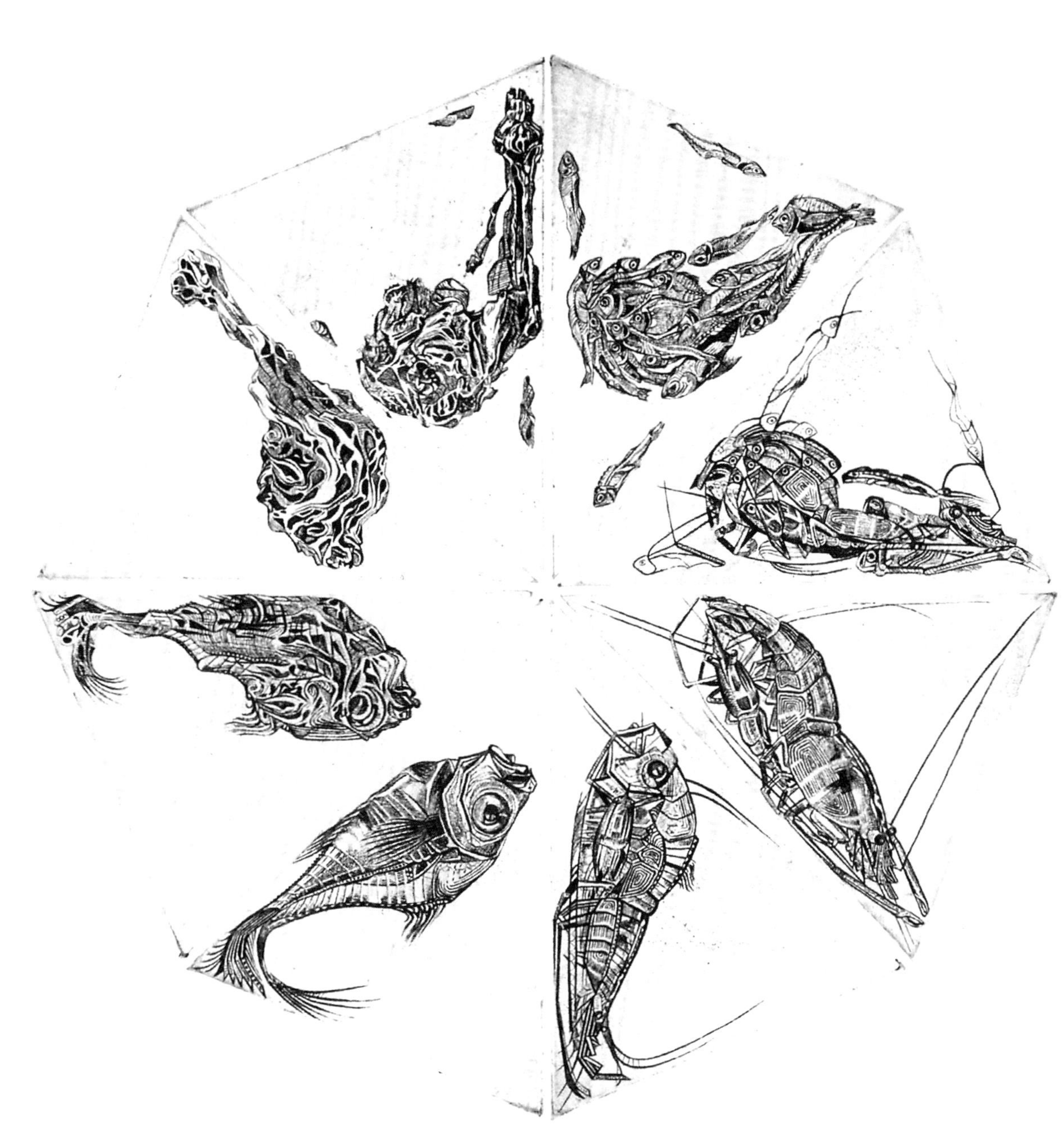

19. Sea Cycle

26 * **Sam**
(p. 16) 1986 165 x 340 mm Edition: 12 Stone lithograph
Prizewinner – Whatman Paper/Printmakers Council Exhibition, Royal Festival Hall, London 1987
Ashmolean Museum & private collections

This was the first of a series of metamorphosing portrait prints in which I attempted to portray somewhat intangible ideas which I felt related to the character traits of each individual – but depicted as sequential narratives to suggest changes in personality over time, rather than portraying just one outward expression of a sitter, frozen in time. I made several detailed pencil drawings of Sam, in Liverpool and in Oxford, as studies for this print.

27 **An Idea**
1986 190 x 125 mm Edition: 12 Stone lithograph
Private collections

28 **Sudesh & Andrea**
1986 60 x 120 mm Not editioned Wood engraving
Private collections

A double portrait of two friends with whom I travelled around India for six weeks in 1986. Nos. 29 – 37 were developed from watercolours and photographs made on this trip.

29 **Lepers begging in New Delhi, India**
1986 85 x 100 mm Not editioned Wood engraving

30 **Keralan Fishermen, India**
1986 75 x 127 mm Not editioned Wood engraving
Private collections

31 **Frogs**
1986 50 x 50 mm Edition: 10 Wood engraving
Ex Libris Museum (Moscow, Russia) & private collections

32 **Carvings of Sacred Cows**
1987 40 x 40 mm Edition: 10 Wood engraving
Ex Libris Museum (Moscow, Russia) collection

33 **Indian Sacred Cow**
1987 55 x 52 mm Edition: 10 Wood engraving
Private collections

34 **Indian Woman becomes Sacred Cow**
1987 120 x 115 mm Not editioned Wood engraving

35 **Kashmiri Boating Woman**
1987 100 x 75 mm Not editioned Wood engraving
Private collections

36 **Indian Palm Tree**
1987 90 x 100 mm Edition: 12 Wood engraving
Ashmolean Museum, Ex Libris Museum (Moscow, Russia) & private collections

37   **Indian Shore Temple, Mahaballipuram**
        1987   150 x 100 mm   Edition: 18   Screenprint
        Private collections

38   **Gina & Jonathan's Wedding**
        1987   60 x 50 mm   Not editioned   Wood engraving
        Private collections
Commissioned for wedding invitation logo.

39   **Tout bien ou rien**
        1987   60 x 37 mm   Unlimited edition   Wood engraving
        Private collections
Ex libris commissioned by Ms Susan Duval.

40   **Angel Cake**
        1987   250 x 100 mm   Edition: 5 A/P's   Perspex engraving
        Private collections
Nos. 40 and 41 were intended to comprise part of a series (which I never pursued) considering the ambiguous, often humorous names we give to recipes. This was also a self-portrait.

41   **Toad in the Hole**
        1987   250 x 145 mm   Edition: 3 A/P's   Perspex engraving
        Private collections

42   **Caveman**
        1987   140 x 80 mm   Edition: 4 A/P's   Etching
        Private collections
This and no. 43 were developed from pencil studies of two small pottery figures which I made in Oxford.

43   **Cavewoman**
        1987   130 x 65 mm   Edition: 3 A/P's   Etching
        Private collections

44   **Hush Little Baby . . .**
        1987   60 x 48 mm   Edition: 15   Wood engraving
        Private collections

45 *   **Tompieme's Daughter**
(p. 16)   1987   85 x 240 mm   Edition: 12   Wood engraving
        Private collections
This sequence grew out of a photograph seen in the Pitt Rivers Museum, Oxford, where I regularly sketched as a student. The photograph showed a small girl holding a wooden spoon on which was carved a stylized portrait of her which, the caption read, had been executed by her father, Tompieme. My image attempted to explore where the humanity in the portrayal of human features ends (if, indeed, it does end) and where a stylized rendition begins. It was also a play on the medium – with both the human child and her wooden likeness (as well as the intermediary stages) being engraved in wood.

46   **Tompieme's Daughter**
        1987   85 x 65 mm   Edition: 10   Wood engraving
        Ex Libris Museum (Moscow, Russia) & private collections
An editioned version of the first engraving of the sequence comprising no. 45.

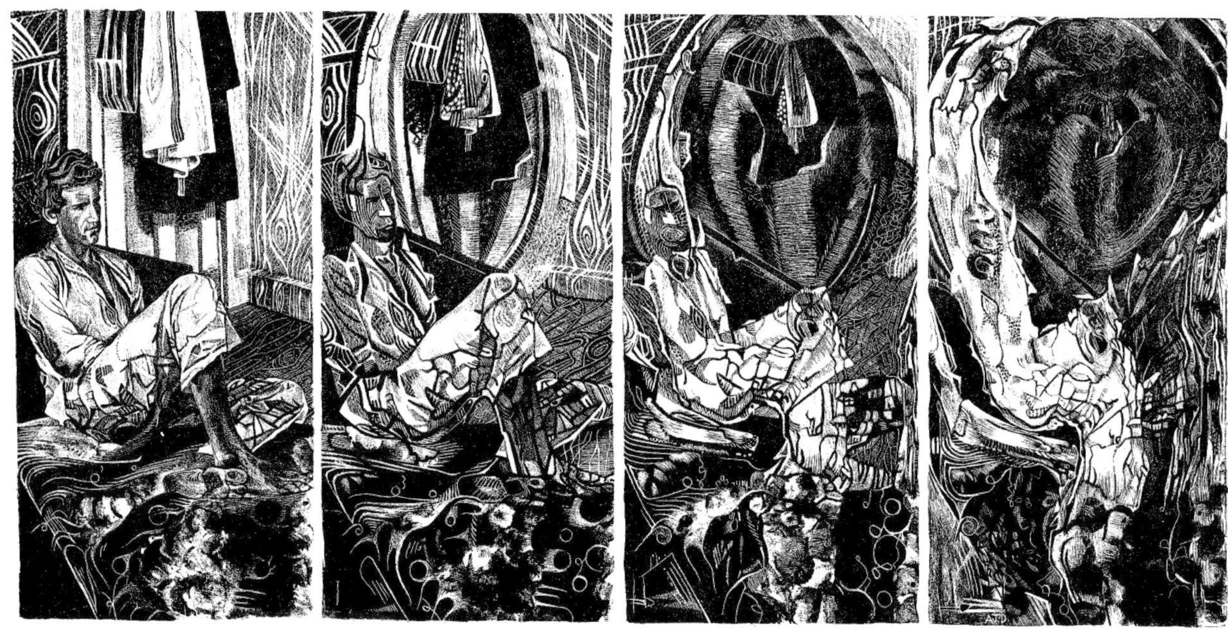

26. Sam

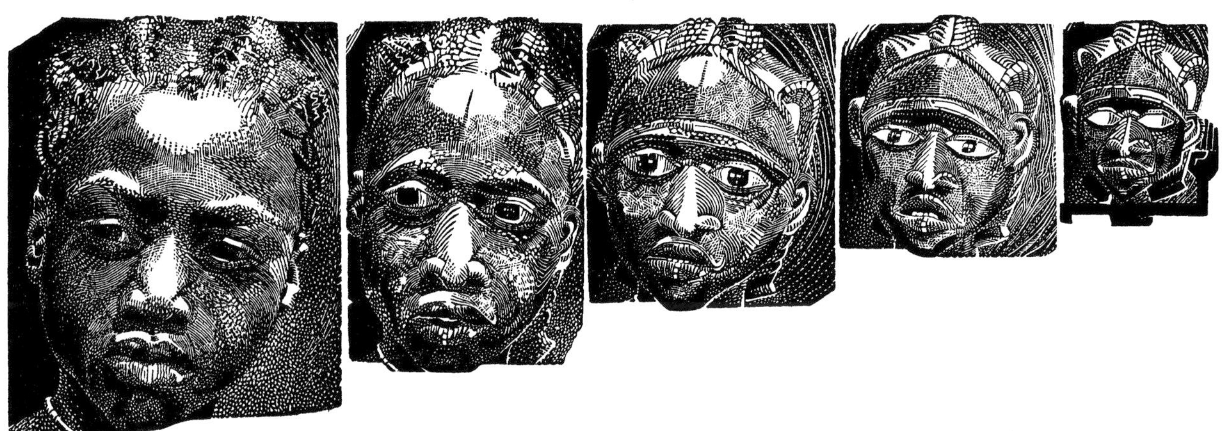

45. Tompieme's Daughter

47 *   **Louis Desmet**

(p. 9)   1987   70 x 56 mm   Edition: 15   Wood engraving

Ex Libris Museum (Moscow, Russia) & private collections

A portrait of my father which was produced from a photograph. (He died when I was nine.)

48   **Charlie**

1987   180 x 350 mm   Edition: 20   Stone lithograph

Private collections

A metamorphosing portrait of a friend in which I perceived him to be rather distant from other people – but happy and independent. I interpreted him as a piece in a jigsaw of humanity. He is completely self-contained within a single piece of the puzzle which fits perfectly into the overall picture but which doesn't overflow into pieces occupied with other figures – all of which spill out of their own prescribed boundaries to intertwine with one another.

49   **Central School of Art & Design**

1988   315 x 320 mm   Unlimited edition   Wood engraving

Ashmolean Museum, Central School of Art & Design (London) & private collections

Commissioned by Central School of Art to illustrate the departments of the School in its final year, before its amalgamation with St Martin's School of Art.

50   **John Dreaming of Lucca**

1988   163 x 385 mm   Edition: 15   Stone lithograph

Ex Libris Museum (Moscow, Russia) & private collections

A metamorphosing portrait of a friend with whom I went to Italy in 1987. This is his daydream of being back in Lucca.

51   **Self-Portraits (based on Piero della Francesca's *Dream of Constantine*)**

1988   570 x 320 mm   Edition: 21   Stone lithograph

A composition based on part of Piero della Francesca's fresco cycle in the church of San Francesco in Arezzo – my favourite piece by this artist – the timeless, serene quality and mathematical precision of whose works are all qualities which I aspire to emulate.

52   **Sam Sleeping**

1988   100 x 150 mm   Edition: 20   Wood engraving

Ex Libris Museum (Moscow, Russia) & private collections

Based on a pencil sketch, this is one of a series of more conventional portraits. (The others are nos. 44, 47, 53, 54 and 55). I regarded them as studies designed to improve my drawing and engraving skills.

53   **John & Jim in the Sunshine**

1988   90 x 70 mm   Edition: 15   Wood engraving

Ex Libris Museum (Moscow, Russia) collection

54   **Jim having a Cup of Tea**

1988   105 x 45 mm   Edition: 15   Wood engraving

Ex Libris Museum (Moscow, Russia) & private collections

55   **Charlie**

1988   60 x 50 mm   Edition: 15   Wood engraving

Ashmolean Museum, Ex Libris Museum (Moscow, Russia) & private collections

56 Mask

| 1988 | 60 x 50 mm | Edition: 21 | Wood engraving |

Ex Libris Museum (Moscow, Russia) & private collections

This and no. 57 were produced for inclusion in no. 58.

57 Tragedy/Comedy

| 1988 | 70 x 250 mm | Edition: 6 | Wood engraving |

58 Book of Masks

| 1988 | 137 x 106 mm (cover size) | Edition: 25 |

Hand-made, concertina-folded, artist's book of wood engravings printed on Basingwerk Parchment
Black cloth covers on front and back printed with two copper engravings

Central School of Art & Design (London) & private collections

A double-sided book which on one side reuses the metamorphosing sequence of no. 45 whilst, on the other, a round red mask, reminiscent of ancient Greek theatre but with the full lips of a buddha, is overprinted with a variety of other masks which each transform it. This was another idea of transformation – of questions of appearance and reality.

59 Giraffes

| 1988 | 75 x 75 mm | Edition: 20 | Wood engraving |

Private collections

60 Perchance to Dream

| 1988 | 175 x 250 mm | Edition: 25 | Wood engraving |

Private collections

Commissioned by Oxford University Press to illustrate *The Young Dragon Book of Verse*.

61 The Marie Celeste

| 1988 | 90 x 100 mm | Edition: 25 | Wood engraving |

Ashmolean Museum, Ex Libris Museum (Moscow, Russia) & private collections

Commissioned by Oxford University Press to illustrate *The Young Dragon Book of Verse*.

62 The Growing Dream

| 1989 | 460 x 300 mm | Edition: 25 | Linocut |

Ashmolean Museum & private collections

The first of a portrait series of five linocuts (nos. 62 – 66) designed to be viewed together as one continuous sequence. My perception of the sitter was of a talented but seemingly directionless man gradually developing some sense of purpose.

63 Awakening

| 1989 | 460 x 300 mm | Edition: 25 | Linocut |

Ashmolean Museum & private collections

64 A Dark Sleep

| 1989 | 460 x 300 mm | Edition: 25 | Linocut |

Ashmolean Museum & private collections

65 Surrounding

| 1989 | 460 x 300 mm | Edition: 25 | Linocut |

Ashmolean Museum & private collections

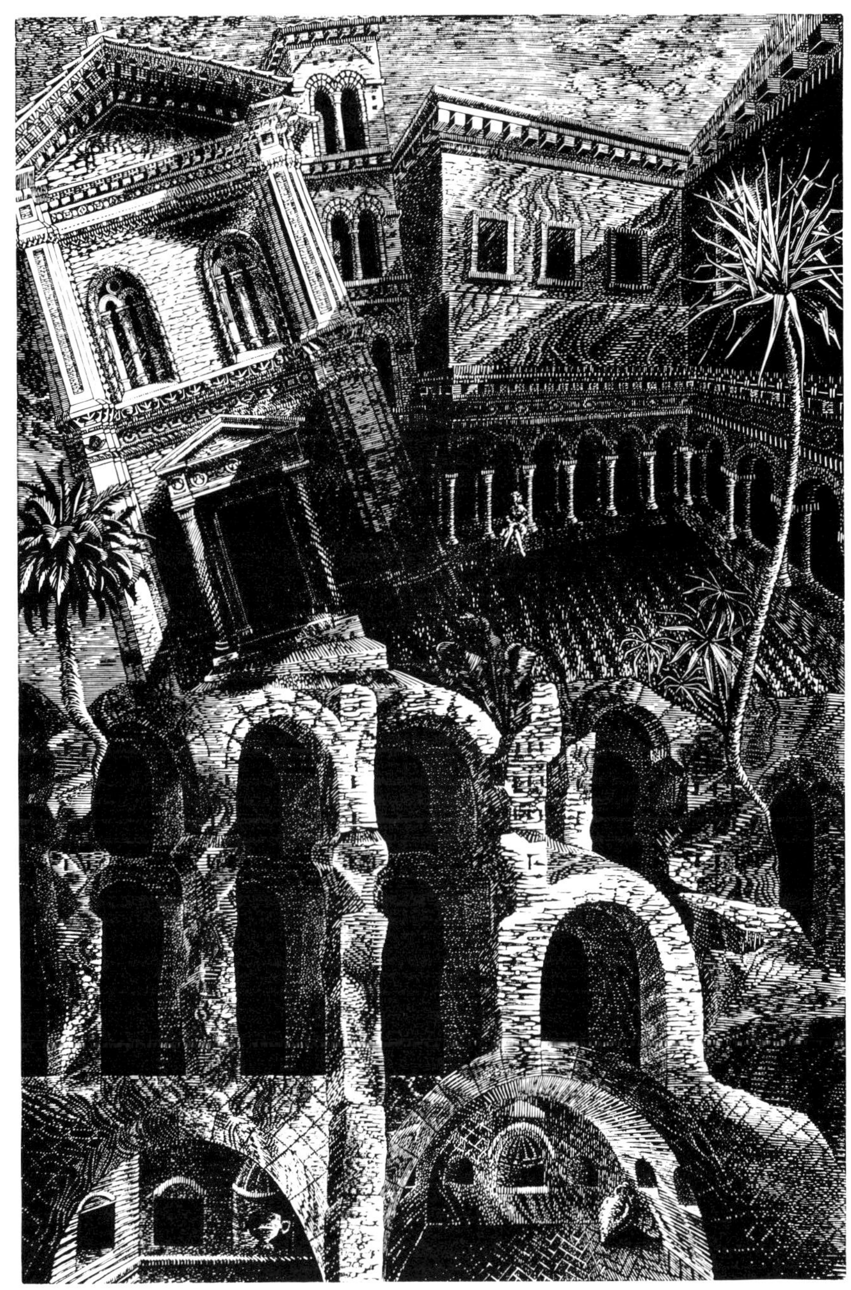

73. Beneath the Surface

66   **Human Buildings**
        1989   460 x 300 mm   Edition: 25   Linocut
                        Ashmolean Museum & private collections

67   **Tom discovering Angels**
        1989   340 x 685 mm   Edition: 10   Three linocuts
                        Private collections
The sitter in this portrait triptych had a strong interest in the art of Cecil Collins and of the Pre-Raphaelites.

68   **Self-Portrait**
        1989   60 x 55 mm   Not editioned   Wood engraving
                        Ex Libris Museum collection (Moscow, Russia)

69   **Masked Mask I**
        1989   480 x 420 mm   Edition: 12   Screenprint
This (and nos. 70 – 72) was commissioned by a London print workshop to reflect a theme of Carnival.

70   **Masked Mask II**
        1989   480 x 420 mm   Edition: 12   Screenprint

71   **Masked Mask III**
        1989   480 x 420 mm   Edition: 13   Screenprint

72   **Masked Mask IV**
        1989   480 x 420 mm   Edition: 12   Screenprint

73 *   **Beneath the Surface**
(p. 19) 1990   600 x 405 mm   Edition: 12   Linocut
                        Ashmolean Museum & private collections
This was my first work started and completed at the British School at Rome. It was based on pencil and wash studies which I made in the city, over a period of months. The print is constructed as a series of layers, in chronological sequence – so, an ancient Etruscan catacomb (beneath the Vatican) supports the ruins of a characteristic but crumbling Roman colonnade (on the Palatine hill) which in turn provides the foundation for a typical medieval cloister and also for the church of Santa Pudenziana (which dates back to c.390 but was rebuilt several times later, notably in 1589). The conjunction of these particular ruins is invented but reflected my ongoing interest in the multi-layered nature of Italian cities where ancient ruins co-exist with or often, literally, comprise part of the fabric or foundations of churches, monuments and apartments built over successive centuries. Sadly, the sketchbook containing all my studies for this and other prints made in Rome was stolen a few days before I returned to London and was never recovered.

74 *   **Progress/Progression?**
(p. 22) 1990   75 x 685 mm   Edition: 32   Wood engraving
                        Ashmolean Museum, Ex Libris Museum (Moscow, Russia) & private collections
I had the idea for the first five of the nine sequential images which make up this image whilst travelling by train from London to Liverpool. The train was passing through mist-covered farmland and I could see the grey shapes of several JCB diggers ripping up earth in a field – but looking more like long-necked animals grazing. I enjoyed the irony between the semblance and reality. My original intention was simply to transform a giraffe into a JCB digger, whilst a tree-filled background would become increasingly depleted as the sequence progressed. I completed the giraffe print (no. 59) in 1988 and took it with me, to Rome, in 1989 – intending to complete the series during the year. It took some two months of sporadic bouts of

engraving to complete as far as the intended last stage of the digger because I was spending most of my time exploring Rome and making sketches. I became fascinated by the huge variety of architecture there – all in varying states of restoration and decay. I also enjoyed the theatricality of the city and the intensity of sunlight and shadow upon its buildings. I decided to extend the series to change the digger into that which it might help to create – an Italianate townscape (but one which might look slightly unreal – like a set for an opera or a painting by de Chirico). On a clear night I also witnessed a lunar eclipse and decided to incorporate this – so that the moon which, in the first five prints of the series, had been gradually waning (to indicate a passage of time) turned into an eclipse in the subsequent four prints. The last image is a view looking out of St Peter's Square which I sketched in the daytime but converted into a nighttime view for this print. Nos. 59, 77, 78 and 79 are editioned versions of individual engravings from this sequence.

When I start on a print series, I make few preparatory drawings for the metamorphosing sections, preferring to work straight onto the blocks, so that, hopefully, each image retains its freshness throughout the time it takes to engrave. For *Progress/Progression?* I worked from a sketch for the cityscape and from drawings, photographs and children's toys for the giraffe and the digger while the other mutating images were developed more or less directly on the blocks.

75   **Development**

     1990   60 x 50 mm   Edition: 21   Wood engraving

     Ex Libris Museum (Moscow, Russia) & private collections

76   **Development** (book)

     1990   134 x 111 mm (cover size)   Edition: 12   Hand-made artist's book of wood engravings printed on Basingwerk Parchment, with linen covers

     Private collections

A concertina-folded artist's book comprising the sequence of no. 74 with no. 75 as a frontispiece. I printed and bound this edition at the British School at Rome.

77   **Progress/Progression? V**

     1990   76 x 76 mm   Edition: 20   Wood engraving

     Private collections

78   **Progress/Progression? VIII**

     1990   76 x 76 mm   Edition: 20   Wood engraving

     Private collections

79   **Rome (Piazza San Pietro)**

     1990   76 x 76 mm   Edition: 20   Wood engraving

     Private collections

80   **Domus Aurea I** (red/brown version)

     1990   405 x 255 mm   Edition: 10   Linocut

     Ex Libris Museum (Moscow, Russia), Slaughter & May & private collections

This and nos. 81, 90 and 91 were produced in Rome and were adapted from sketches of the magnificent Domus Aurea in Rome – the golden house of Nero which lies beneath the Esquiline Hill. The sketches were made from memory immediately after a guided tour there which was conducted by torchlight in semi-darkness.

81   **Domus Aurea II** (red/brown version)

     1990   405 x 255 mm   Edition: 10   Linocut

     Ex Libris Museum collection (Moscow, Russia)

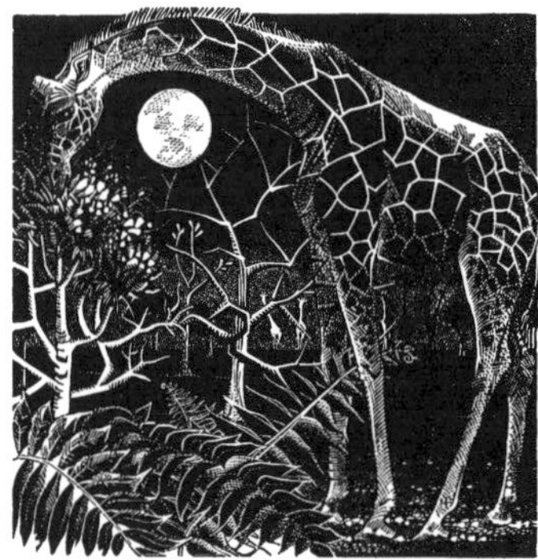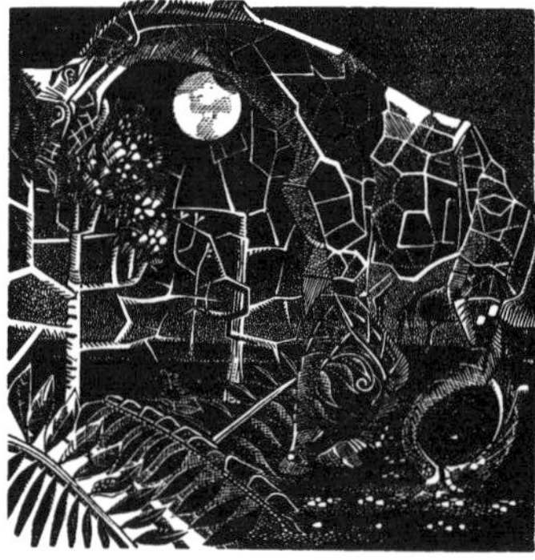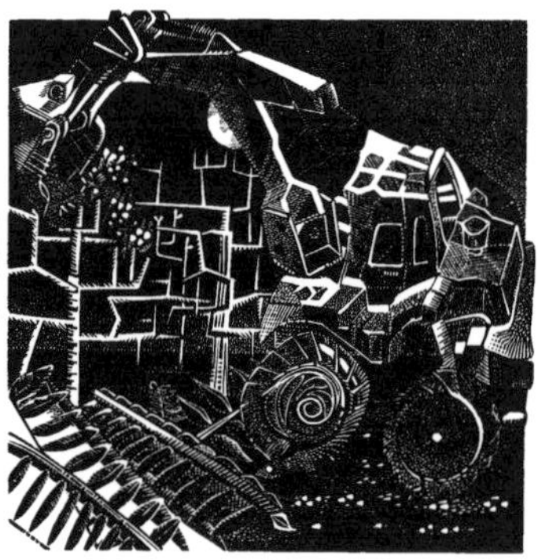
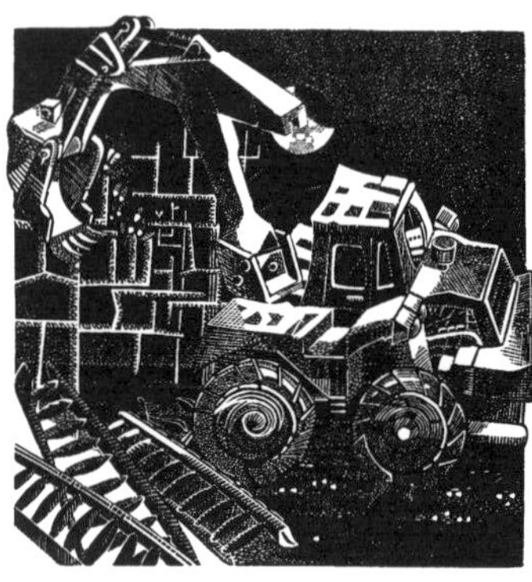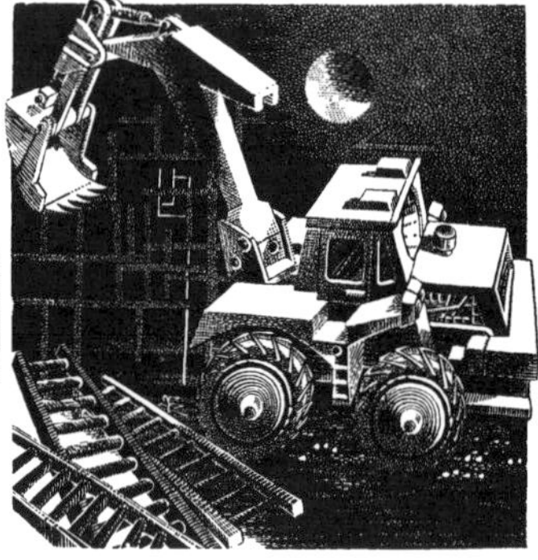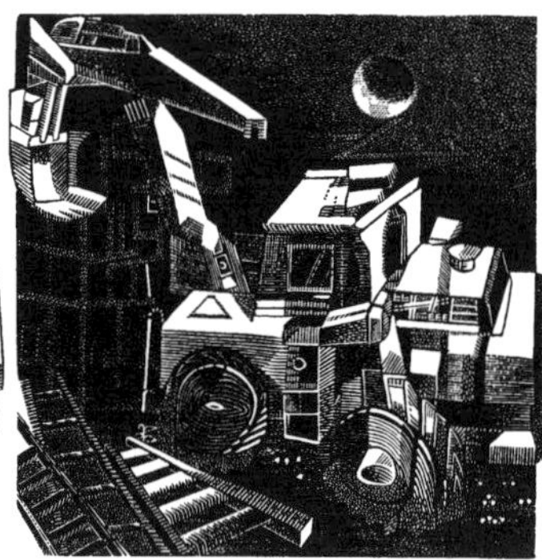
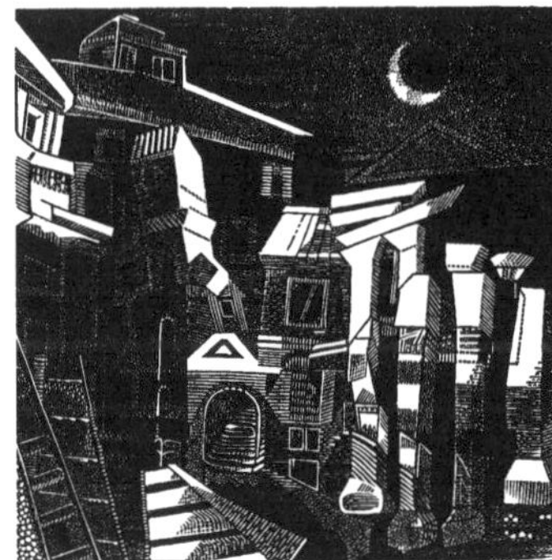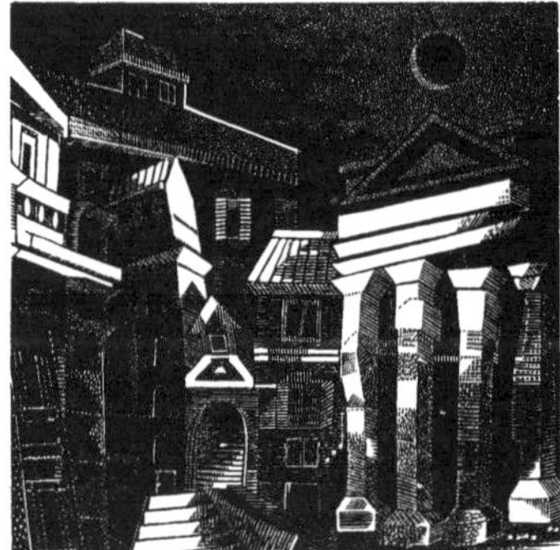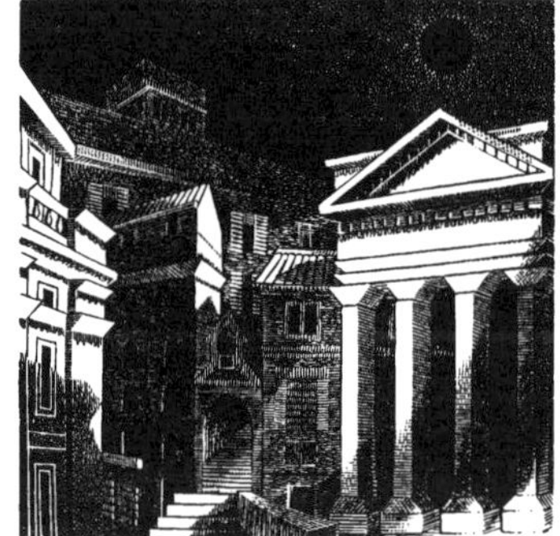

74. Progress/Progression?

*(This image is reproduced here in three sections; as an editioned print
it is a series of nine engravings printed in a single horizontal line)*

82 * **Self-portrait**

(p. 44)   1990   205 x 55 mm   Edition: 5   Collaged wood engraving
            Ashmolean Museum & private collections

The germ of the idea for this, my first collage, arose by accident. I had taken the engraving block of no. 68 with me to Rome in order to print a few experimental copies in black, rather than in the red/orange in which I had editioned it. I did not like the reprints so tore them up. Later, when I was clearing up the day's printing mess, I noticed the torn shreds on the floor and was struck by the new form and pattern they had acquired as fragments. The finished collage, in which I interleaved black and red/orange torn versions of the engraving, is structured rather less randomly than the initial happy chance which gave rise to it.

83 * **Torre**

(p. 25)   1990   215 x 160 mm   Edition: 1   Wood engraving & collage
            Private collection

My second collage (also produced in Rome) turned out to be the first of an ongoing series of images of towers. It consists of collaged fragments of multiple impressions from some of the blocks which comprise no. 74. It reflects an interest in images of the biblical Tower of Babel (such as those by Pieter Bruegel) and also impressions of Rome's architecture.

84 **Italian Hill Town**

            1990   75 x 75 mm   Edition: 1   Wood engraving & collage
            Ashmolean Museum collection

My third collage (produced on my return to London) is an imaginary town largely composed of bits of a mutating ladder (from some of the engravings comprising no. 74). It is intended to suggest a hill town, such as the old town of Salerno, in southern Italy, where repeated earthquakes have damaged the foundations of many buildings and where houses and shops along each narrow alley are braced apart by crude timber girders – to prevent their collapse.

85 **Torre II**

            1990   80 x 70 mm   Edition: 1   Wood engraving & collage

This was created as a companion piece to no. 84 and is intended to convey something of the steep, often stepped, winding roadways of an Italian hill town, with a suggestion of scaffolding and ladders to convey the fragility of the buildings at the summit. It is composed of bits of nos. 74 and 75.

86 **Folding/Unfolding**

            1990   115 x 420 x 25 mm   Edition: 1   Wood engraving, linocut & collage

This image combined a metamorphosing subject with an intriguing pleated paper construction – to contrast the seemingly weighty architecture with the semi-transparent, tissue-thin folding screen on which it is presented. I wanted it to have the appearance of a delicate boxed book. The collage is made of bits of nos. 73 and 74 with black and white versions of no. 36.

87 **Italy 3 a.m.**

            1990   48 x 247 mm   Edition: 1   Wood engraving, linocut & collage
            Private collection

This image reflects fantasy rather than reality (but with echoes of Roman aqueducts or amphitheatres) and its title relates both to its being an image about the night hours – and also to the fact that it was completed at 3 a.m. one morning. It is composed largely of elements of nos. 17 and 74.

88 **Building on Buildings**

            1990   440 x 345 mm   Edition: 1   Linocut, wood engraving & collage
            Private collection

A collage with a similar theme and aspect to that of no. 73. Parts of it are, in fact, composed from proofs of that linocut.

89 * **Il Colosseo**

(p. 28)   1990   185 x 125 mm   Edition: 1   Wood engraving, collage
           Ashmolean Museum collection   & grey ink wash

I produced this collage whilst I was artist-in-residence at Oriel 31 (the Davies Memorial Gallery), Newtown, Powys, Wales in autumn 1990. It was based on photographs and the memory of studies of Rome's Colosseum in my stolen sketchbook. It is made, largely, from fragments of no. 74.

90   **Domus Aurea I** (blue version)
      1991   405 x 255 mm   Edition: 12   Linocut
      Private collections

91   **Domus Aurea II** (blue version)
      1991   405 x 255 mm   Edition: 12   Linocut
      Ashmolean Museum & private collections

92   **Autumn & Spring**
      1991   22 x 216 mm   Edition: 15   Wood engraving
      The Times, Ex Libris Museum (Moscow, Russia) & private collections

Commissioned by The Times newspaper.

93   **Property**
      1991   30 x 35 mm   Edition: 10   Wood engraving & linocut
      The Times & Ex Libris Museum (Moscow, Russia) collections

Commissioned by The Times newspaper.

94   **Instruments**
      1991   30 x 35 mm   Edition: 10   Wood engraving & linocut
      The Times & Ex Libris Museum (Moscow, Russia) collections

Commissioned by The Times newspaper.

95   **Theatre**
      1991   30 x 35 mm   Edition: 10   Wood engraving & linocut
      The Times, Ex Libris Museum (Moscow, Russia) & private collections

Commissioned by The Times newspaper.

96   **Gardening**
      1991   30 x 35 mm   Edition: 10   Wood engraving & linocut
      The Times, Ex Libris Museum (Moscow, Russia) & private collections

Commissioned by The Times newspaper.

97   **Eating Out**
      1991   30 x 35 mm   Edition: 10   Wood engraving & linocut
      The Times & Ex Libris Museum (Moscow, Russia) collections

Commissioned by The Times newspaper.

98   **Stately Homes**
      1991   30 x 35 mm   Edition: 10   Wood engraving & linocut
      The Times & Ex Libris Museum (Moscow, Russia) collections

Commissioned by The Times newspaper.

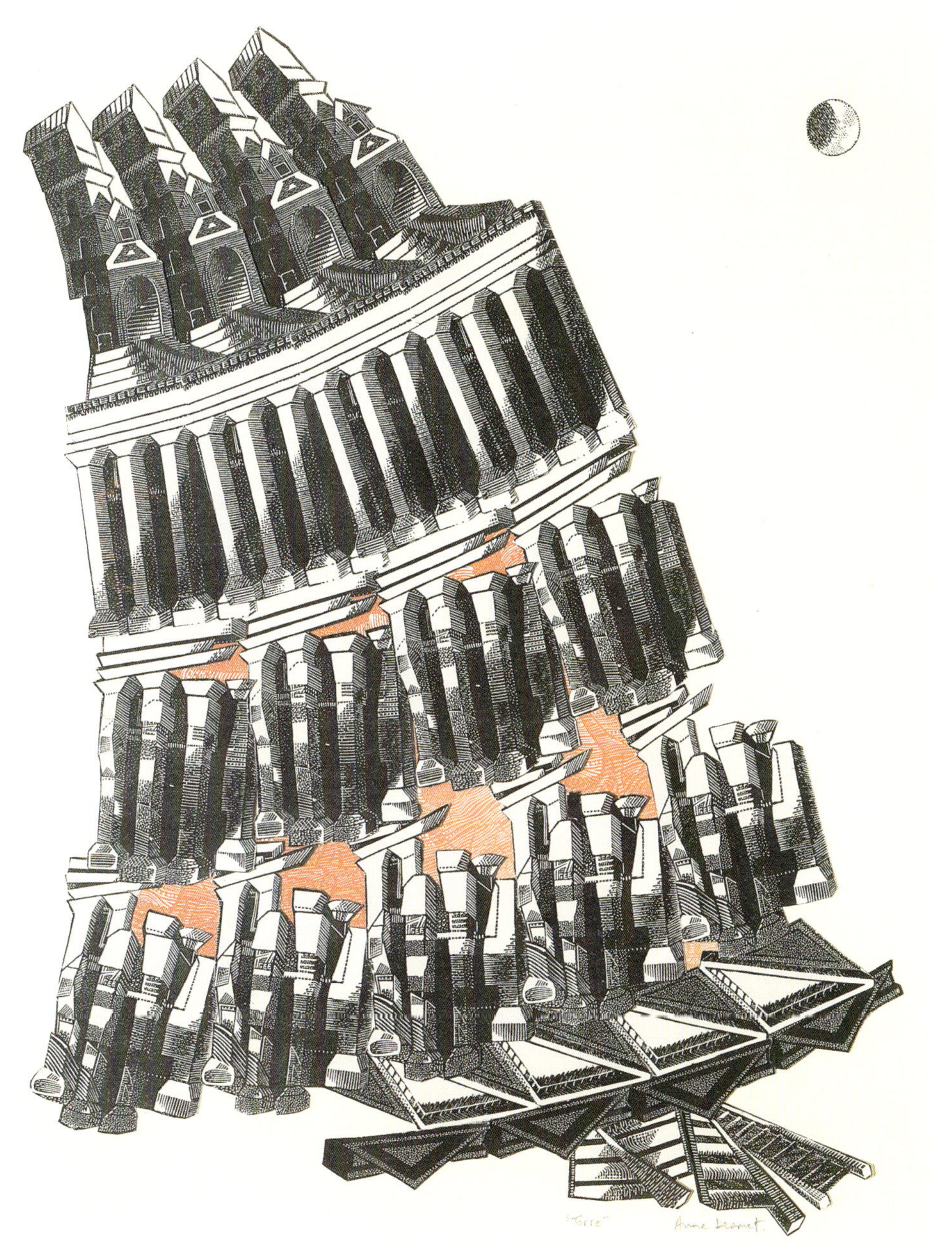

83. Torre

99   **TV**

| | | | |
| 1991 | 30 x 35 mm | Edition: 10 | Wood engraving & linocut |

The Times, Ex Libris Museum (Moscow, Russia) & private collections

Commissioned by The Times newspaper. The figure watching TV is a self-portrait.

100   **Narrow Boats**

| 1991 | 30 x 35 mm | Edition: 10 | Wood engraving & linocut |

The Times, Ex Libris Museum (Moscow, Russia) & private collections

Commissioned by The Times newspaper.

101   **Shopping**

| 1991 | 30 x 35 mm | Edition: 10 | Wood engraving & linocut |

The Times & Ex Libris Museum (Moscow, Russia) collections

Commissioned by The Times newspaper.

102   **Colosseum**

| 1991 | 80 x 95 mm | Edition: 40 | Wood engraving |

Ex Libris Museum (Moscow, Russia) & private collections

Engraved on a circular piece of boxwood, this image was adapted from aerial views on postcards as well as from my own photographs and studies of the Colosseum – the shape of which I modified slightly to fill the block. This image has been a vital component in the construction of a large number of my collages.

103 *   **A Slice of Rome**

(p. 32)   1991   160 x 220 mm   Edition: 10   Linocut with collaged wood engraving

Private collections

As well as enjoying the circular shape of the Colosseum, I was also interested in the diamond shape created by its surrounding road systems. The roads are depicted in a reduction linocut using three colours printed on white paper; the Colosseum itself is printed (from the engraving block used for no. 102) in deep blue, onto a creamy-beige Japanese paper. I cut around the outlines of these prints of the Colosseum and collaged them onto the linocut prints of the road network, to create the completed editioned prints. The components of this edition were printed on an old Victorian nipping press – as were nos. 92 – 102, 108, 115, 117, 118 and 121.

104   **Calder Valley**

| 1991 | 76 x 51 mm | Edition: 10 | Wood engraving |

Private collections

105   **Calder Valley II**

| 1991 | 76 x 51 mm | Edition: 10 | Wood engraving |

106   **Calder Valley III**

| 1991 | 76 x 51 mm | Edition: 10 | Wood engraving |

107   **Hebden Bridge**

| 1991 | 76 x 51 mm | Edition: 10 | Wood engraving |

108   **A Second Development**

       1991   76 x 200 mm   Edition: 27   Wood engraving

Ashmolean Museum, Ex Libris Museum (Moscow, Russia) & private collections

This metamorphosing series of four engravings (also editioned as individual images: nos. 104 – 107) is based on pen and wash sketches made of Hebden Bridge and its environs in autumn 1990. The idea was to suggest the increasing encroachment of housing developments onto the rural landscape and to indicate the way in which that landscape is being irrevocably changed over time. It is, however, intended to provoke reflection rather than making any definite political statement about the rights and wrongs of the issue.

109   **A Collection of Columns**

       1991   80 x 370 x 13 mm   Edition: 1   Wood engraving, coloured Japanese
                  Private collection   tissues, glass-headed pins & collage

An imaginary colonnade of what might be the result of the haphazard reassembling of unearthed fragments from an archaeological excavation. The last few columns intentionally toy with scale – they might be bird tables perched on miniature pilasters or possibly a human-scale dwelling for St Simeon Stylites.

110   **Hebden Bridge**

       1991   145 x 95 x 25 mm   Edition: 1   Wood engraving, coloured
                  Private collection   Japanese tissues & collage

A three-dimensional collage using folded, reassembled fragments from no. 108 to create an idea of landscape seen from above, but with ambiguities as to whether you are looking at angular ploughed fields or a collection of tiled roofs.

111   **Italian Triptych**

       1991   50 x 330 mm   Edition: 1   Wood engraving, linocut & collage
                  Private collection

A development of the nighttime atmosphere of no. 87 using components of no. 74 in its construction.

112 *   **Leaning Tower**

(p. 45)   1991   515 x 145 mm   Edition: 1   Wood engraving, linocut,
                                                       stone lithograph, coloured
                                                       Japanese tissues & collage

                Prizewinner – Royal Overseas League Annual Open Exhibition, London 1991
                Private collection

This is intended to recall the Leaning Tower of Pisa (which I have never actually seen). It is constructed from multiple proofs of no. 102, some of which were printed on white paper and some on a mustard-coloured Japanese paper. I cut around the outlines of these printings and collaged them onto an off-white Japanese paper. The (linocut) palm tree is a device to provide a sense of space. The column in the foreground which props the tower is a collaged fragment of no. 25.

113   **Hillside or Harbour**

       1991   102 x 96 x 4 mm   Edition: 1   Wood engraving, watercolour,
                  Private collection   linocut & collage

An invented view composed of repeated elements from no. 74. The ascending sweep of buildings seemed to suggest a hill town, but the girder-like structures beneath could be either huge foundations or the industrial docks and cranes of a commercial port.

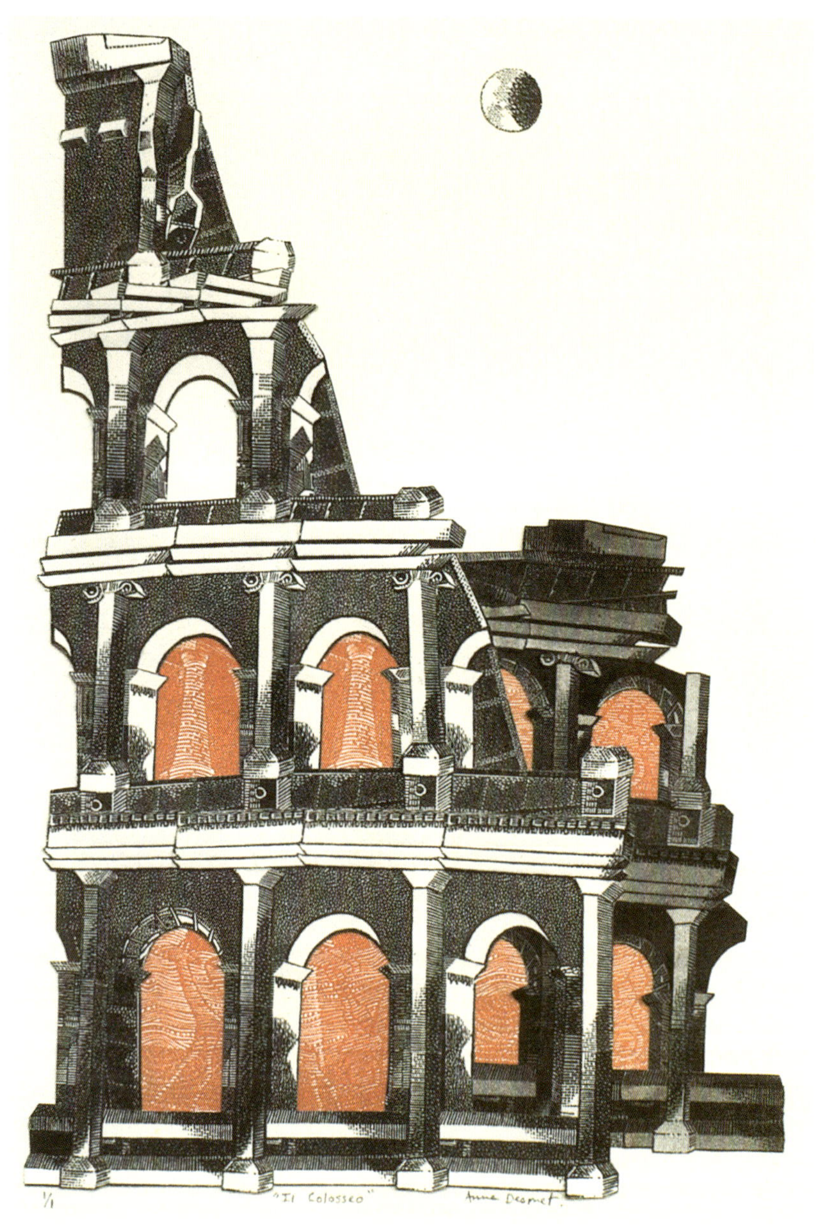

89. Il Colosseo

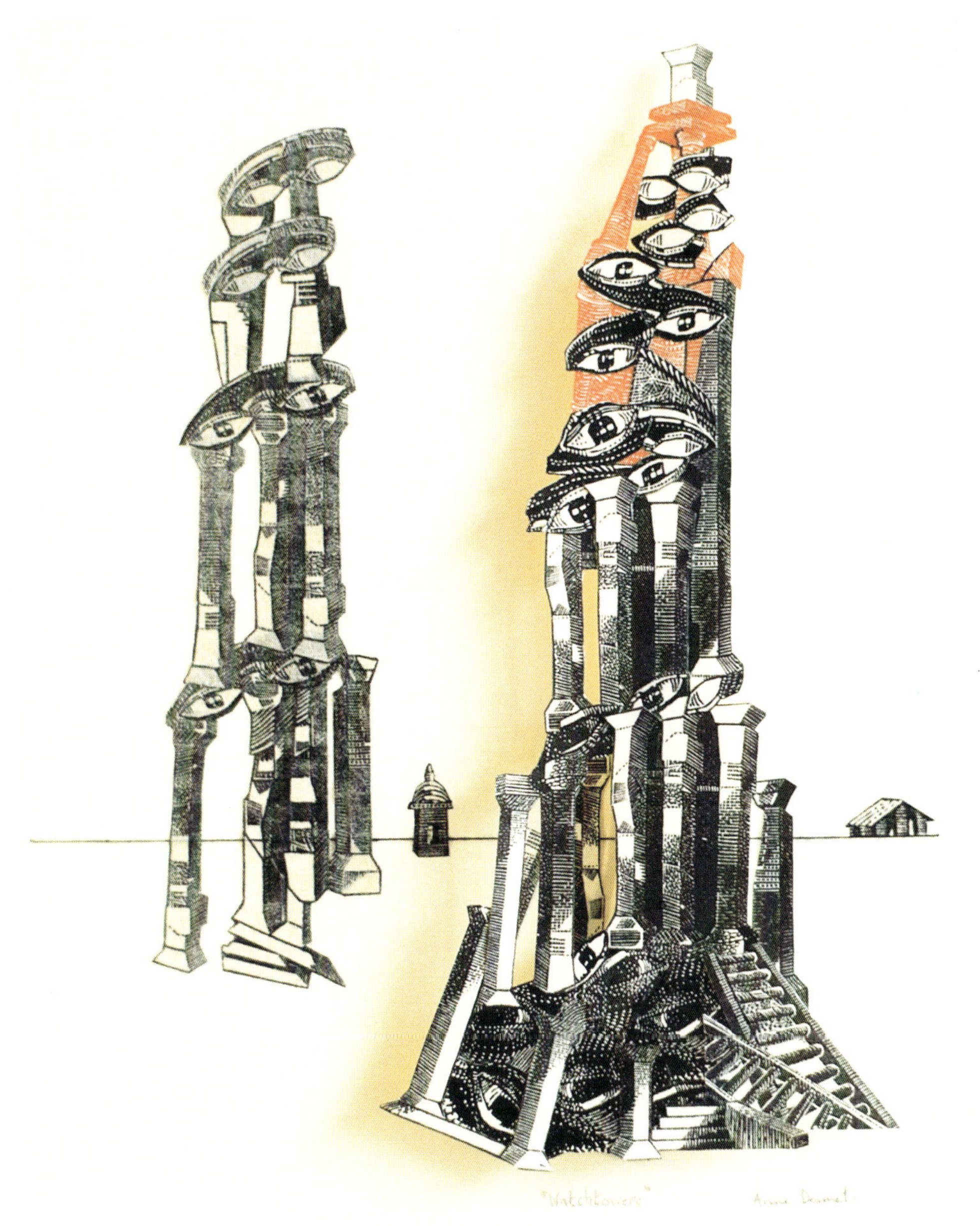

132. Watchtowers

114 **Ideal City**

| 1991 | 90 x 320 x 3 mm | Edition: 1 | Wood engraving & collage |

Private collection
with glass-headed pins

This was created by four printings of no. 79 printed side by side, but with the first and the third printing impressed onto the reverse of the paper which is an almost transparent Japanese tissue. The areas of colour were created by collaging tiny pieces of coloured Japanese papers onto the white backing sheet onto which the print is pinned, so that colours show through the semi-transparent tissue of the print. The resulting image suggests a formal, mathematically plotted townscape. The idea for this image came from the panel painting, *Ideal City*, by a collaborator of Piero della Francesca, which hangs in the National Gallery (the Ducal Palace) at Urbino.

115 **Ski Slopes**

| 1992 | 28 x 114 mm | Edition: 20 | Wood engraving |

The Times, Ex Libris Museum (Moscow, Russia) & private collections

Commissioned by The Times newspaper.

116 **10 Engravings** (editioned with all 10 images printed on one sheet of paper)

| 1992 | 95 x 245 mm | Edition: 10 | Wood engravings |

The Times collection

Commissioned by The Times newspaper.

117 **Venus x 2**

| 1992 | 33 x 27 mm | Edition: 15 | Wood engraving |

The Times, Ex Libris Museum (Moscow, Russia) & private collections

Commissioned by The Times newspaper.

118 * **Bergamo (fragments)**

(p. 3)

| 1992 | 285 x 82 mm | Edition: 25 | Collaged wood engraving |

Ashmolean Museum & private collections

I engraved the components of this engraving on several blocks of varying shapes and sizes which were then printed on white Japanese paper. I then tore carefully around the outside edge of each image and reassembled the pieces like a jigsaw puzzle by collaging them onto an off-white Japanese paper. The image is based on a pencil, grey wash and watercolour drawing I made of this view in 1991 and the final print is intended to suggest fragments of, perhaps, an ancient fresco.

119 **Pompeii**

| 1992 | 73 x 47 mm | Edition: 20 | Wood engraving |

Ex Libris Museum (Moscow, Russia) & private collections

An editioned detail of no. 120.

120 * **Reconstructing the Ruins**

(p. 8)

| 1992 | 432 x 45 mm | Edition: 40 | Wood engraving |

Ashmolean Museum & private collections

A sequence of thirteen interlocked images exploring the passage of time in architectural terms, using Italian motifs: a 1st Century Pompeian grotto supports a Roman temple; rising above these are Luccan and Bergamascan 12th Century churches, then a 13th Century church with campanile. Above these is the High Renaissance chapel of San Pietro in Montorio by Bramante and then churches of the 15th/16th Centuries. Surmounting all is a Baroque lantern tower rising into a stormy sky. The print is intended to be read either as a celebration of the progressive achievements of architects and builders (yet with hints of the Tower of Babel) or as an archaeological search exploring the riches of the past and affirming their relevance to the present.

121   **Corinthian Column**

    1992   30 x 17 mm   Edition: 15   Wood engraving
               Private collections

122   **Reconstructing the Ruins** (book)

    1992   93 x 88 mm (cover size)   Edition: 15   Hand-made artist's book of wood
                                                    engravings printed on Basingwerk
                                                    Parchment, with cloth covers

        Ashmolean Museum, National Art Library at the Victoria & Albert Museum,
        Manchester Metropolitan University Library & private collections

A concertina-folded artist's book comprising the sequence of no. 120. The frontispiece is composed of no. 121 with two collaged moons – waxing and waning – from no. 74. The moons are intended to suggest the passage of time – a device suggested by a novel in woodcuts, *Madman's Drum* (Jonathan Cape Ltd, 1930) by Lynd Ward, which I greatly admire.

123 *   **Roma**

(p. 51)   1992   610 x 200 mm   Edition: 20   Linocut
               Prizewinner – South Bank Picture Show, Royal Festival Hall, London 1992
               Ashmolean Museum, Ex Libris Museum (Moscow, Russia) & private collections

A print developed in London from a small but detailed pencil and wash study of the rooftops of Rome which I made over three days at New Year, 1991, from the roof terrace of a small hotel off Campo dei Fiori.

124   **City within Tent**

    1992   585 x 343 mm   Edition: 1   Stone lithograph, linocut, wood
               Private collection   engraving, black ink & collage

A collage playing with ideas of scale, light and perspective and composed primarily of small architectural details from nos. 73, 74, 81 and 118 collaged onto a proof of no. 51.

125 *   **Reflection**

(p. 40)   1992   170 x 330 x 5 mm   Edition: 1   Wood engraving, linocut, Japanese
                                                    tissues, gold paper, glass-headed pins
               Private collection   & collage

This image was created in the same way as no. 114 and develops the same ideas. It uses eight printings of no. 78 printed alternately on the front and back of the paper to create a townscape and its apparent reflection in water. This work also includes collaged fragments from proofs of nos. 74 and 118.

126 *   **Il fiume e i ponti**

(p. 36)   1992   220 x 170 x 6 mm   Edition: 1   Wood engraving, coloured Japanese
               Private collection   tissue, black ink & collage

Loosely based on a postcard of an aerial view of Florence's Ponte Vecchio, this composition, however, also tries to chart something of the passage of a river from town into countryside. The architecture and landscape are composed of sections of nos. 74 and 108 modified with black pen and collaged onto a semi-transparent sheet of Japanese tissue. Coloured patterns or reflections in the river, along with sections of bridge which appear to be below the waterline, were created by collaging engraved fragments and blue wrappers from Italian *Amaretti* biscuits onto the reverse side of this semi-transparent tissue.

127   **Degeneration**

    1992   140 x 760 x 20 mm   Edition: 1   Wood engraving, coloured
                                                      Japanese paper & collage

A further development of the three-dimensional structures of nos. 86 and 109 with a theme of environmental mutation. An invented townscape (composed of details of nos. 74 and 118) gradually implodes to form a compact heap of rubble which in turn gradually shrinks and fuses to form a solid ball of dense matter – or perhaps a full stop.

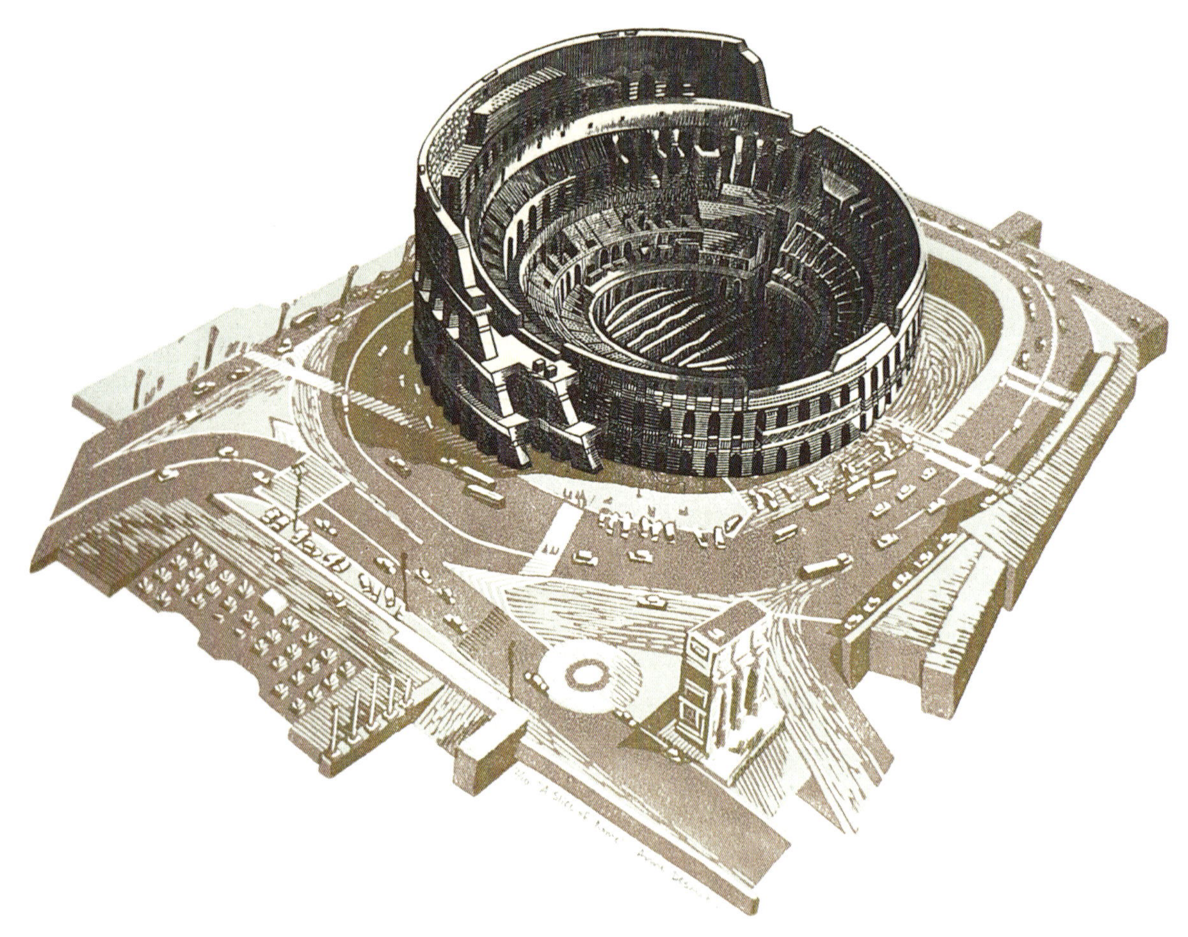

103. *A Slice of Rome*

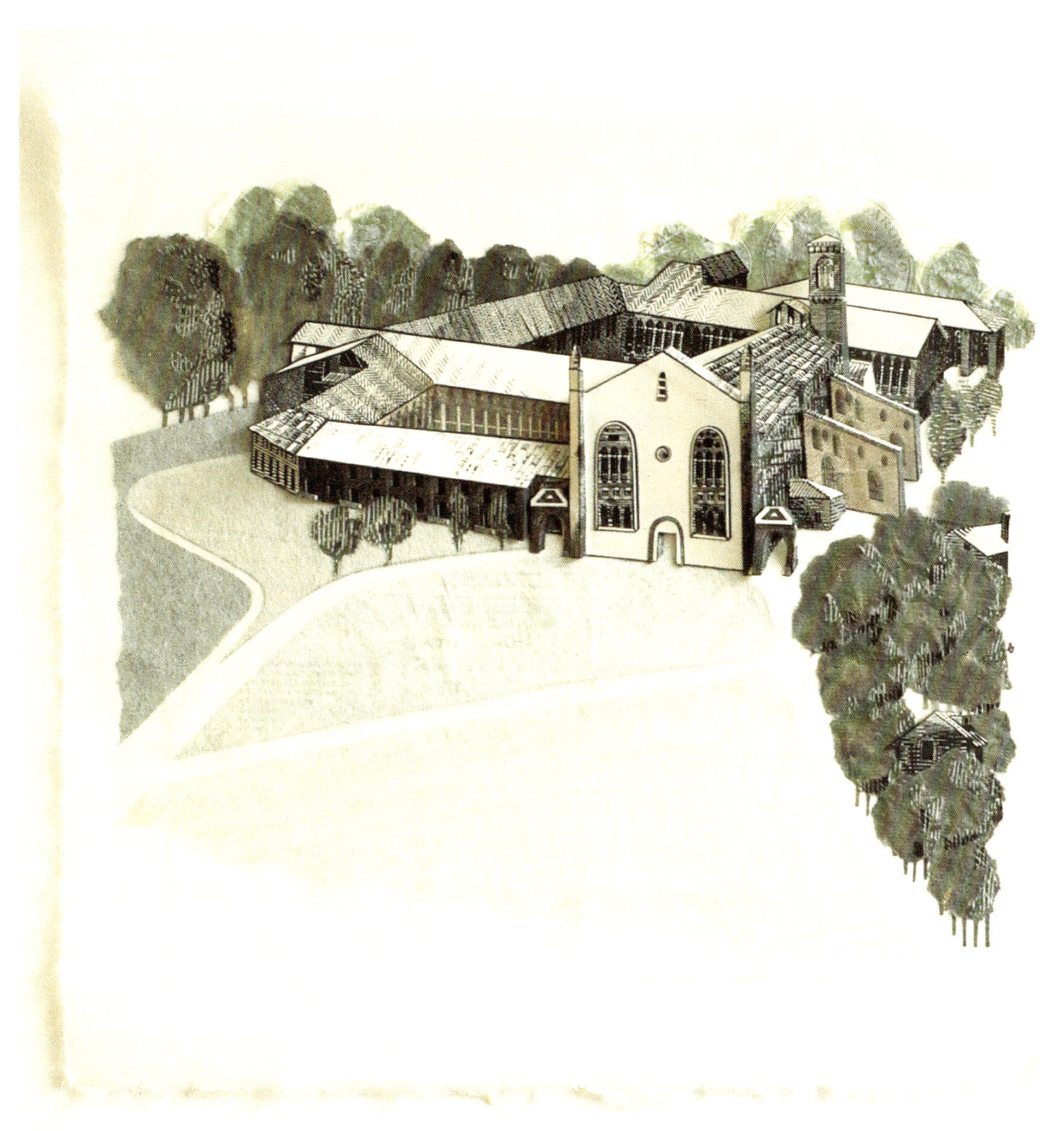

130. Chiesa di S. Agostino, Bergamo

128 Teatro di Marcello, perhaps

       1992   406 x 483 mm   Edition: 1   Linocut, wood engraving, coloured
Japanese papers & collage

A collage composed primarily of combined repeated forms from nos. 73, 74, 118 and 123. The building is an imaginary structure but with echoes of Rome's Theatre of Marcellus combined with Bruegel's *Tower of Babel*.

129 Torre III

       1992   725 x 510 mm   Edition: 1   Wood engraving, linocut, graphite,
       Victoria & Albert Museum collection   Japanese tissue & collage

A further development of the *Tower of Babel* theme composed primarily of combined repeated elements from nos. 73, 118 and 123, collaged onto off-white Japanese paper. The illusion of cast shadows from the tower and palm trees was created by a combination of collaged *Amaretti* wrappers and coloured Japanese papers blended with graphite.

130 * Chiesa di S. Agostino, Bergamo

(p. 33)   1992   255 x 255 x 12 mm   Edition: 1   Wood engraving, linocut, Japanese
                Private collection   tissue, pencil & collage

Based on a pencil sketch I made, looking from a hill in 1991, down at the church below, I was interested in creating a strong sense of this aerial view (as in no. 110) by making this collage in three dimensions. The church and cloisters are made primarily of highly modified, cut, folded and reassembled elements of nos. 74 and 118, with added pencil details and bits of an Italian banknote.The trees are coloured, torn, Japanese tissue collaged with fragments of *Amaretti* wrappers and bits of proofs (printed in green ink)of nos. 80 and 81. The foreground comprises coloured Japanese papers, additional bits of green printings of nos. 80 and 81 and stripes of archival tape – all collaged onto the back of the semi-transparent tissue on which the collage is constructed so that their shapes and colours show through the front in a muted form.

131 I Monumenti

       1992   76 x 460 mm   Edition: 1   Wood engraving, black ink,
                Private collection   Japanese tissue & collage

A triptych comprising three views, collaged from details of nos. 74, 108 and 118. The buildings are loosely based on architecture seen, sketched and photographed in Rome, Florence and Siena but their compositional combination is invented. It is a daytime sequel to nos. 87 and 111.

132 * Watchtowers

(p. 29)   1992   165 x 140 x 7 mm   Edition: 1   Wood engraving, cotton thread & collage
                Private collection

This collage, in low-relief, combines elements of nos. 45, 74, 75 and 118. The seed of the idea grew from a half-remembered poster on the London Underground which involved many unblinking eyes staring out from the paper.

133 * 21st Century Christmas Tree

(p. 52)   1992   197 x 127 mm   Edition: 1   Wood engraving, coloured
                Private collection   Japanese tissue & collage

Created from combined repeated elements from no. 74, this tree is intended to suggest the negative potential results of global deforestation as well as the positive aspects of recycling to create new, extraordinary structures. The idea came from a piece in an exhibition of art made entirely from recycled objects which was shown at the Royal Festival Hall, London, some years ago. One exhibit was a small life-size tree made primarily from the amputated limbs of broken dolls.

134 * Roma dal Aventino
(p. 51)   1993   610 x 203 mm   Edition: 30   Linocut
Ashmolean Museum, Ex Libris Museum (Moscow, Russia) & private collections

This linocut is developed from a detailed pencil and grey wash drawing which I made in 1992. It (and all my subsequent prints to date) was printed on an 1859 Hopkinson and Cope Albion press which was installed in my studio in late 1993.

135   Temple of Vesta
1993   102 x 100 mm   Edition: 20   Wood engraving
Musée d'Art Contemporain (Chamalières, France) & private collections

136   Rotunda
1993   82 x 70 mm   Edition: 15   Wood engraving
Private collections

137   Rotunda III
1993   84 x 70 mm   Edition: 30   Wood engraving
Private collections

138 * Rotunda x 4
(p. 55)   1993   102 x 332 mm   Edition: 40   Wood engraving
Private collections

I engraved this metamorphosing sequence on four separate blocks. It is a passage, in four steps, through many centuries of history – from Rome's 2nd Century B.C. Temple of Vesta (now reattributed to Hercules Victor) to a modified version of Oxford's neo-classical Radcliffe Camera. I substituted the small dome of the Camera for the larger dome of Rome's church of S. Andrea della Valle (17th Century). Nos. 135 – 137 are editioned individual blocks from this sequence.

139   Sicilia
1993   127 x 73 mm   Edition: 40   Wood engraving
Ex Libris Museum (Moscow, Russia) & private collections

A view (developed from a pencil and wash drawing made in 1992) of the railway station serving Taormina – seen from above – from the public gardens of the town itself.

140   The Bibles of William Tyndale
1993   41 x 53 mm   Edition: 20   Wood engraving
The Times, Ex Libris Museum (Moscow, Russia) & private collections

Commissioned by The Times newspaper.

141   Abbey School logo
1993   32 x 38 mm   Not editioned   Wood engraving & plasticard
The Abbey School & Ex Libris Museum (Moscow, Russia) collections

Commissioned by The Abbey School, Gloucestershire.

142   New House
1993   75 x 45 mm   Edition: 20   Wood engraving
Ex Libris Museum (Moscow, Russia) & private collections

A view of my home in London (a 19th Century terraced house) engraved shortly after I moved in, depicting it whilst it was undergoing refurbishment.

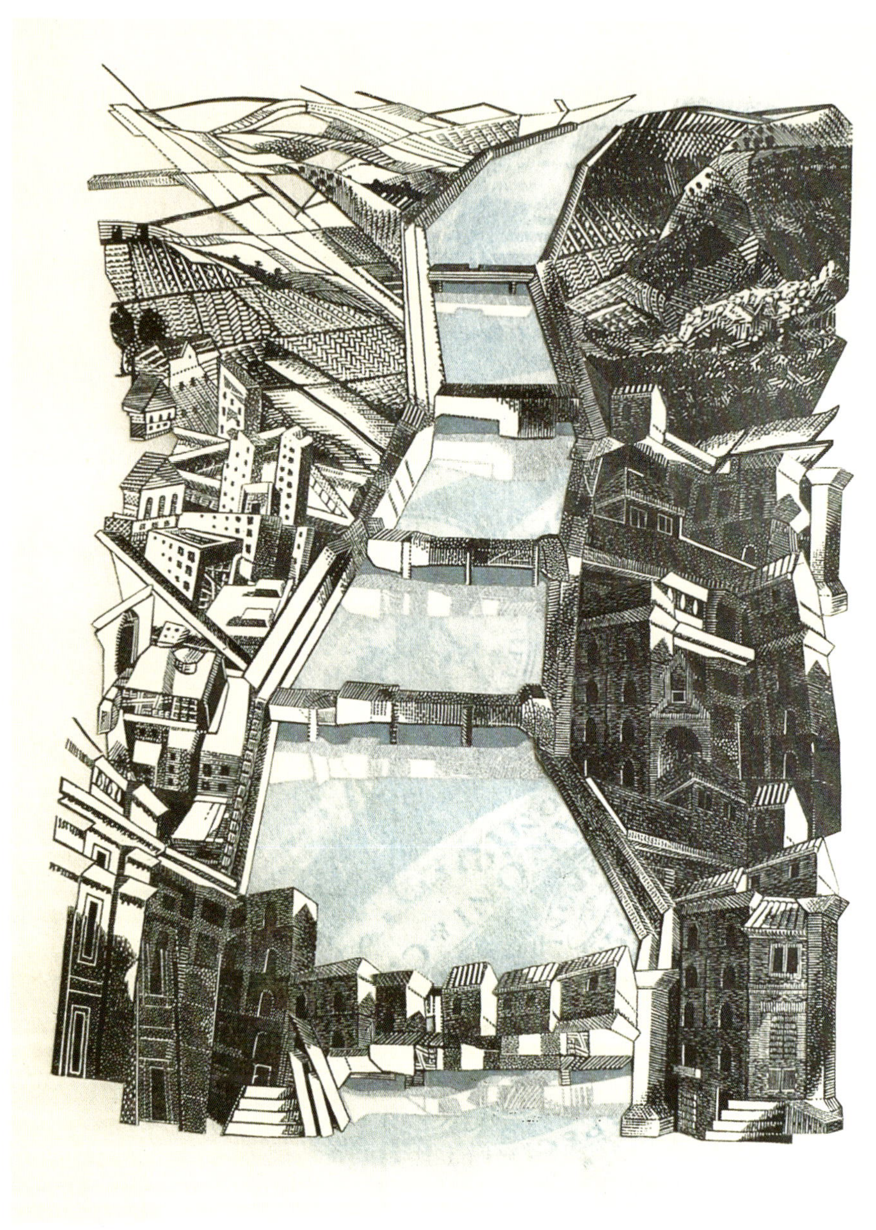

126. *Il fiume e i ponti*

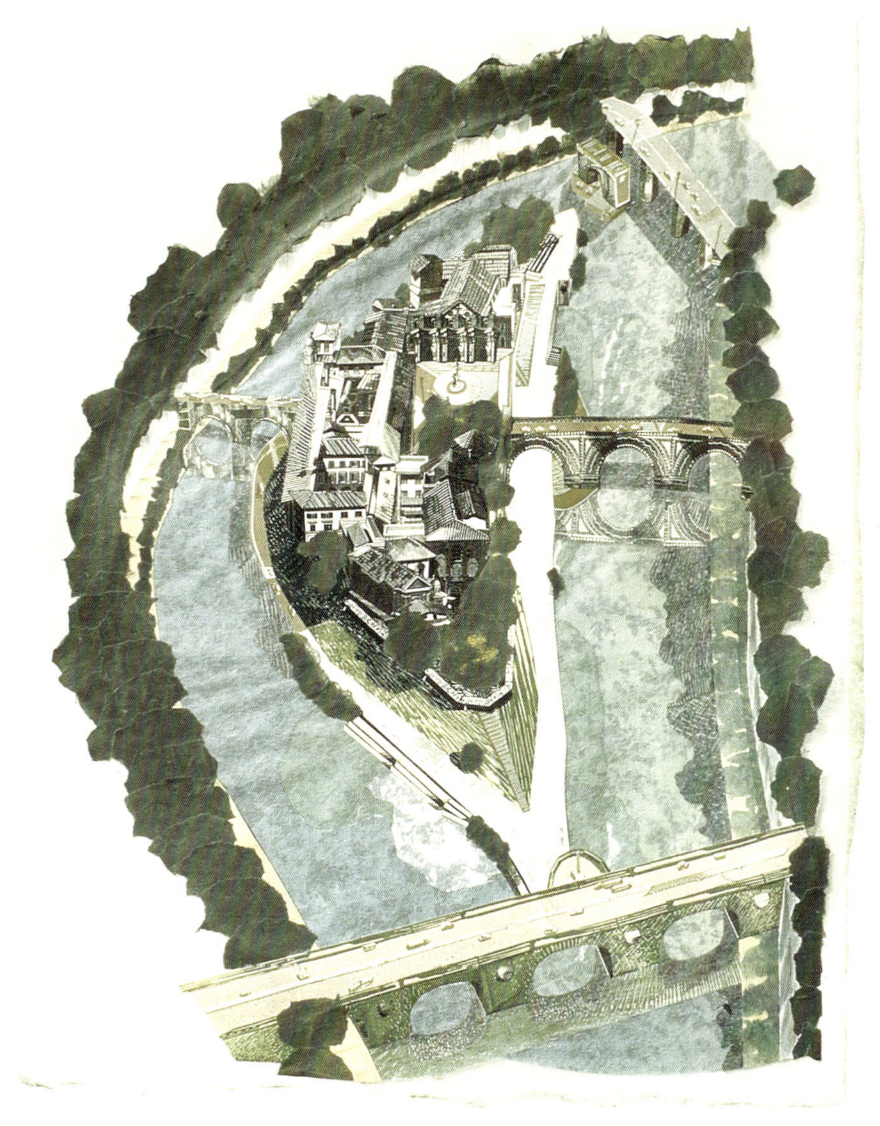

186. Isola Tiberina

143	**Venice**			
	1994	63 x 65 mm	Edition: 20	Wood engraving
		Private collections		

| 144 | **Teatro Greco** | | | |
| | 1994 | 50 x 67 mm | Edition: 20 | Wood engraving |

145	**Building Blocks II**			
	1994	44 x 44 mm	Edition: 10	Wood engraving
		Private collections		

| 146 | **Building Blocks III** | | | |
| | 1994 | 44 x 44 mm | Edition: 10 | Wood engraving |

| 147 | **Building Blocks IV** | | | |
| | 1994 | 44 x 44 mm | Edition: 10 | Wood engraving |

| 148 | **Building Blocks V** | | | |
| | 1994 | 44 x 44 mm | Edition: 10 | Wood engraving |

| 149 | **Building Blocks VI** | | | |
| | 1994 | 44 x 44 mm | Edition: 10 | Wood engraving |

| 150 | **Building Blocks VII** | | | |
| | 1994 | 44 x 44 mm | Edition: 10 | Wood engraving |

| 151 | **Building Blocks VIII** | | | |
| | 1994 | 44 x 44 mm | Edition: 10 | Wood engraving |

| 152 | **Building Blocks IX** | | | |
| | 1994 | 44 x 44 mm | Edition: 10 | Wood engraving |

| 153 | **Building Blocks X** | | | |
| | 1994 | 44 x 44 mm | Edition: 10 | Wood engraving |

| 154 | **Building Blocks XI** | | | |
| | 1994 | 44 x 44 mm | Edition: 10 | Wood engraving |

| 155 | **Building Blocks XII** | | | |
| | 1994 | 44 x 44 mm | Edition: 10 | Wood engraving |

| 156 | **Building Blocks XIII** | | | |
| | 1994 | 44 x 44 mm | Edition: 10 | Wood engraving |

| 157 | **Building Blocks XIV** | | | |
| | 1994 | 44 x 44 mm | Edition: 10 | Wood engraving |

| 158 | **Building Blocks XV** | | | |
| | 1994 | 44 x 44 mm | Edition: 10 | Wood engraving |

159 * **Building Blocks** (details illustrated on cover)

    1994   787 x 65 mm   Edition: 40   Wood engraving

Prizewinner – RWA Open Print Exhibition, Bristol 1994

Ashmolean Museum, Ex Libris Museum (Moscow, Russia) & private collections

Nos. 143–158 are editioned, individual components of this complete metamorphosing sequence of sixteen sequential engravings which make a journey through time and across Italy. They start with the remains of a 1st Century Sicilian amphitheatre (at Taormina) which comes to resemble a building site and then the site machinery itself: bulldozers, trucks and steamrollers. These gradually reverse the process of decline until they have created an 18th Century Venetian church. The sequence is a reflection on both the negative and positive aspects of a developing "civilisation". Does the advance of the modern world ignore and destroy the culture of the past or does it build a better world by taking the best that history can offer? These two views are echoed by the juxtaposition of Venice and its cosmopolitan diversity with Sicily's insularity, while it is also intended to hint at the current political and social relationship of northern Italy to the south.

160   **Re-development**

    1994   8 x 62 mm   Edition: 30   Wood engraving

Ex Libris Museum (Moscow, Russia) & private collections

161   **A Building Book**

    1994   83 x 128 mm (cover size)   Edition: 20   Hand-made artist's book of wood engravings printed on Zerkall paper, with cloth covers

Private collections

A concertina-folded artist's book comprising the sequence of no. 159. The frontispiece is composed of no. 160.

162   **Forum**

    1994   76 x 100 mm   Edition: 50   Wood engraving by Anne Desmet & Roy Willingham

Ex Libris Museum (Moscow, Russia) & private collections

This composition was based on a pencil sketch of Roy's and a pen sketch of mine (both made at New Year, 1991) as well as photographs and postcards of Rome's forum. The architectural background was largely engraved by me, whilst the more abstract foreground was mainly engraved by Roy. We created this engraving to illustrate our wedding invitations.

163   **Hills & Valleys, Dawn to Dusk**

    1994   165 x 470 x 5 mm   Edition: 1   Wood engraving, black ink, coloured Japanese papers, gold leaf, glass-headed pins & collage

This image was produced by six printings of no. 139 printed side by side, but with the first, third and fifth printing being impressed onto the reverse of the paper which is an almost transparent Japanese tissue. The areas of colour were created as in nos. 114 and 125. Pinpoints of light on or from the buildings were created with minute pieces of gold leaf. The image is intended to be read from left to right, to suggest the passage of a day – from the misty, creamy tones of early morning, to midday and afternoon with a stronger, amber light and the hills showing a brighter green, through to sunset with pink hues reflected in the lake-water and a blue-grey dusk bathing the hillside as lights begin to twinkle in houses in the valley.

164   **Late Night Reflection**

    1994   203 x 292 x 3 mm   Edition: 1   Wood engraving, coloured Japanese papers, gold leaf, black ink & collage

Private collection

A further development of the themes of nos. 114 and 125 using collaged details from nos. 118, 120 and 159.

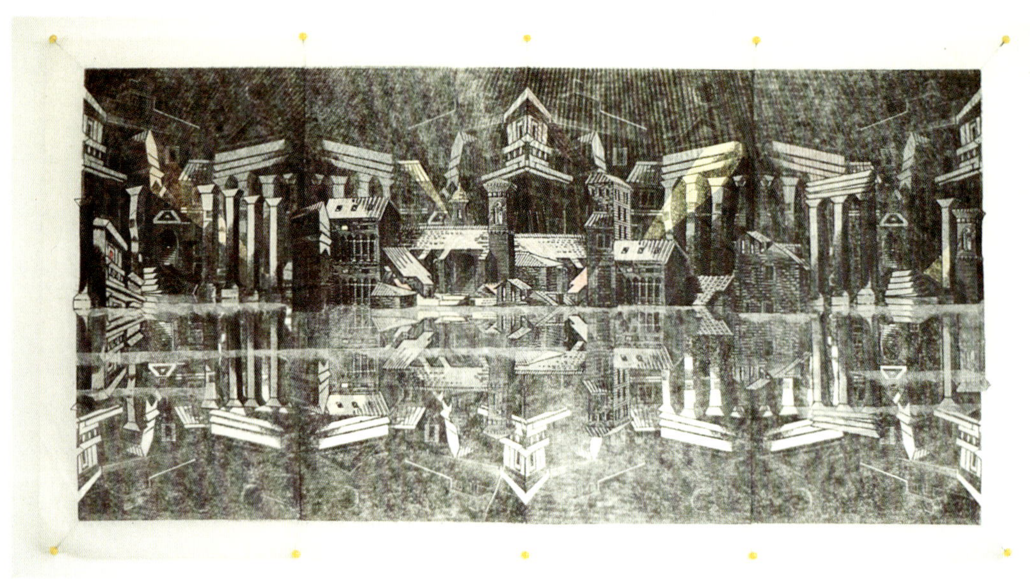

125. Reflection

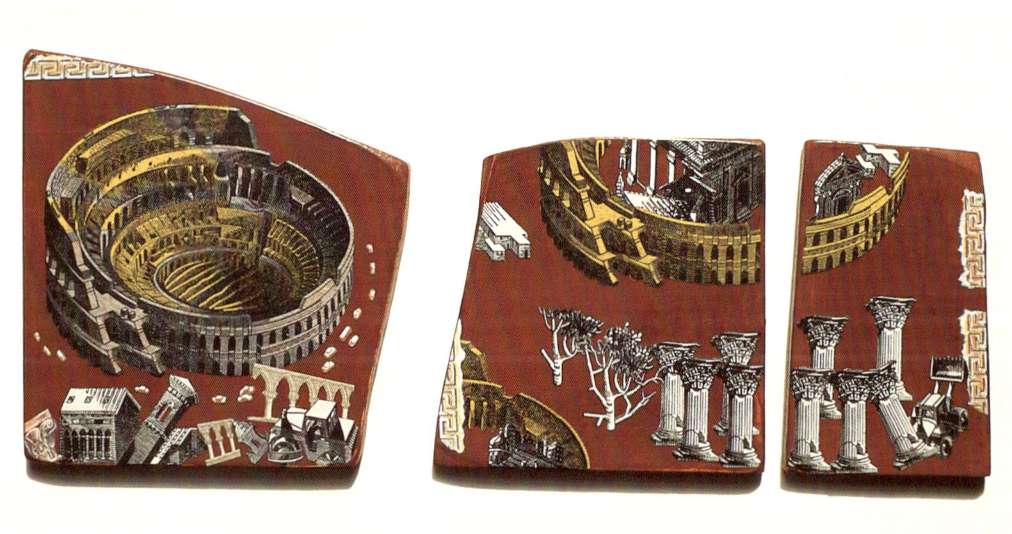

189. Building the Viale Foro Imperiale

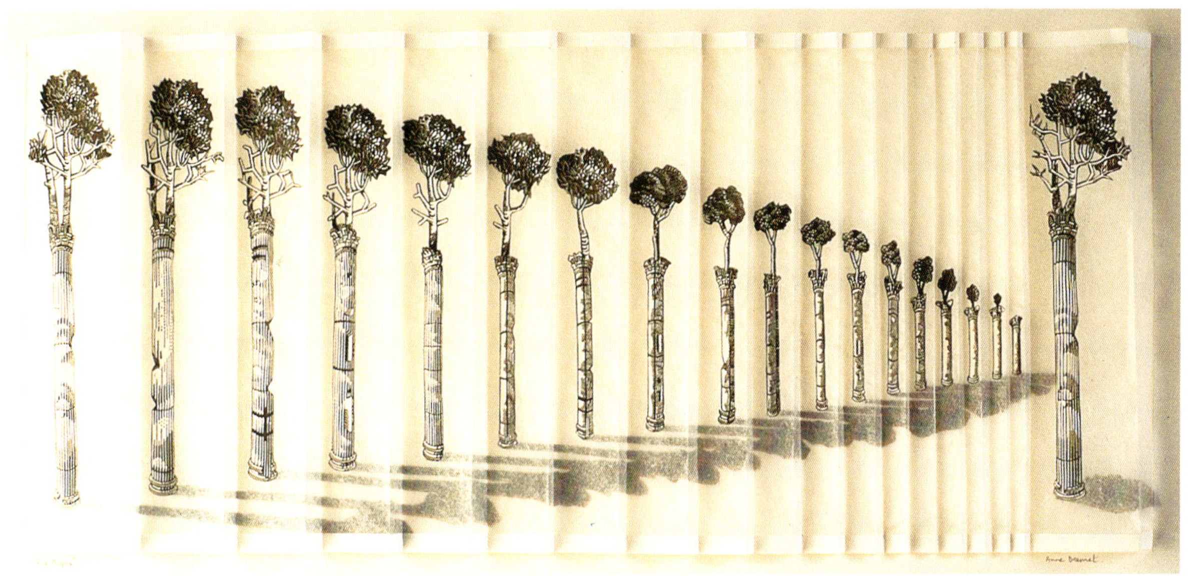

174. Via Appia

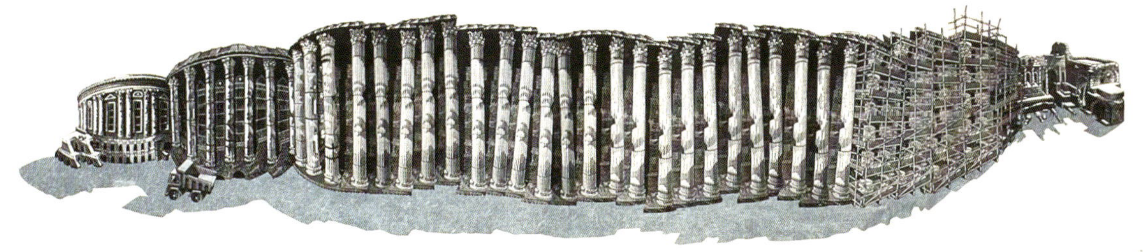

173. In restauro

165 Empire Building

| 1994 | 108 x 308 mm | Edition: 1 | Linocut, wood engraving, |
| | *Private collection* | | coloured pencil & collage |

A collage comprising nine images which are designed to be read like a sequence of film-stills, charting a progression over time. The vignette, which gradually becomes cluttered with cars and colonnades, is based on the Arch of Constantine in Rome. Its basis is a detail of successive proofs of no. 103.

166 Five Fragments

| 1994 | 83 x 417 mm | Edition: 1 | Wood engraving, coloured Japanese |
| | | | papers, black ink & collage |

A collage of five vignettes of characteristic but invented Italian landscape and architecture – created primarily from collaged details from nos. 108, 118, 135, 139, 159 and 162.

167 Icon

| 1994 | 219 x 219 x 3 mm | Edition: 1 | Wood engraving, gold paper, black ink, |
| | *Private collection* | | coloured Japanese papers & collage |

This piece and nos. 168 and 169 were invented compositions of Italian church architecture (created from details of nos. 120, 138 and 159) intended to suggest the beauty, fragility and timelessness of jewel-like medieval altarpieces.

168 Altarpiece

| 1994 | 228 x 241 x 2 mm | Edition: 1 | Wood engraving, coloured Japanese |
| | *Private collection* | | papers, black ink & collage |

A development of the theme of no. 167 incorporating fragments of nos. 118, 120 and 159.

169 Triptych

1994	219 x 219 x 18 mm	Edition: 1	Wood engraving, coloured Japanese
			papers, gold paper, plastic beads,
			cotton thread, black ink & collage

A development of nos. 167 and 168 with the image (composed of bits of nos. 74, 120, 138 and 159) actually taking the three-dimensional form of a miniature triptych.

170 Predella

1994	159 x 584 x 2 mm	Edition: 1	Wood engraving, coloured pencil,
			gold leaf, coloured Japanese papers,
	Private collection		black ink & collage

A development of the theme of nos. 167, 168 and 169, this is constructed largely from proofs of nos. 118, 120, 138 and 159.

171 Inner City

1994	203 x 597 x 2 mm	Edition: 1	Wood engraving, coloured Japanese
			papers, black ink, cotton thread,
	Private collection		plastic beads & collage

Composed of fragments of nos. 74, 118, 120, 138 and 159, this is a development of the format of no. 170 but I endeavoured to create a stronger illusion of three dimensions by positioning trees, columns and some buildings onto a stage-like foreground (in the manner of Paolo Uccello's *Battle of San Romano*) and using collaged strips of coloured Japanese paper to simulate cast shadows from these "props".

172   Internal City

      1994   560 x 750 mm   Edition: 1   Stone lithograph, linocut, wood
      Private collection   engraving, gold leaf, black ink & collage

This continues a theme of the altarpiece and develops ideas in no. 124. It is composed primarily of small architectural details from nos. 73, 118, 123, 134, 138 and 159 collaged onto a proof of no. 51.

173 *   In restauro

(p. 41)   1994   152 x 673 mm   Edition: 1   Wood engraving, Japanese tissue,
              Private collection   coloured paper & collage

An invented, colonnaded monument composed of repeated forms from nos. 138 and 159. The building is seen partly clad in scaffolding, undergoing restoration, as are so many of Italy's ancient monuments. It could also be some sort of strange mutating caterpillar emerging from its chrysalis.

174 *   Via Appia

(p. 41)   1994   170 x 406 x 14 mm   Edition: 1   Wood engraving, coloured Japanese
                                                        papers, archival paper tape & collage

A development of the structural form of nos. 86, 109 and 127 to create an impression of Rome's Via Appia with crumbling columns receding into the distance. The collage is constructed from repeated elements from nos. 59, 74 and 138. The illusion of cast shadows from the colonnade was created by collaging coloured Japanese papers onto the backing sheet behind the semi-transparent concertina-folded paper on which the collage is constructed.

175   Illuminations

      1994   93 x 705 mm   Edition: 1   Wood engraving, pencil, gold leaf,
      Private collection   Indian coloured paper & collage

Seven tiny vignettes of Italianate buildings and views collaged onto a red-brown Indian paper. The buildings are largely manipulated fragments of nos. 74, 118, 120, 138, 139 and 159. The sequence is intended to recall Indian miniatures or medieval illuminated manuscripts.

176 *   Self-portrait with Towers

(p. 45)   1994   736 x 203 mm   Edition: 1   Wood engraving, Japanese tissue
               Private collection   & coloured paper, pencil & collage

A variation on the theme of no. 112, this image was suggested by both Pisa's leaning tower and Venice's Scala del Bovolo. It is constructed from multiple proofs of no. 135, some of which were printed on white and some on off-white Japanese paper. I cut around modified outlines of these printings and collaged them onto another off-white paper. The other towers and churches provide a sense of space and distance. The pencil-drawn self-portrait was intended to provoke a sense of the grandeur and sheer physical presence of some of Italy's greatest edifices, next to which a person might be an ant.

177   Electric Cable

      1994   220 x 308 mm   Edition: 1   Wood engraving, pencil,
      The National Grid Collection   coloured pencil & collage

Commissioned by the National Grid plc.

178 *   Balliol College, Oxford

(p. 5)   1995   165 x 246 mm   Edition: 250   Wood engraving
      Ashmolean Museum, Balliol College, IMG Corporate (New York, USA) & private collections

Edition commissioned by Balliol College – based on sketches and photographs made, from the college's tower, in 1994.

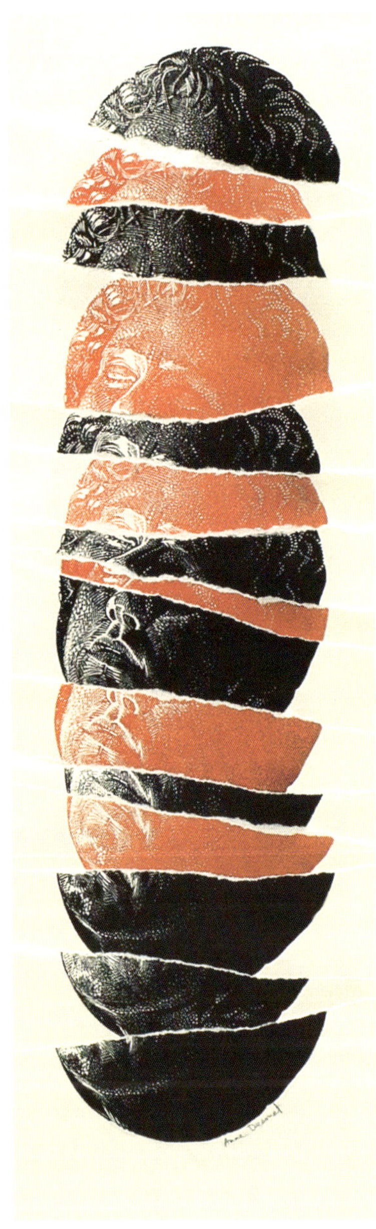

82. Sef-portrait

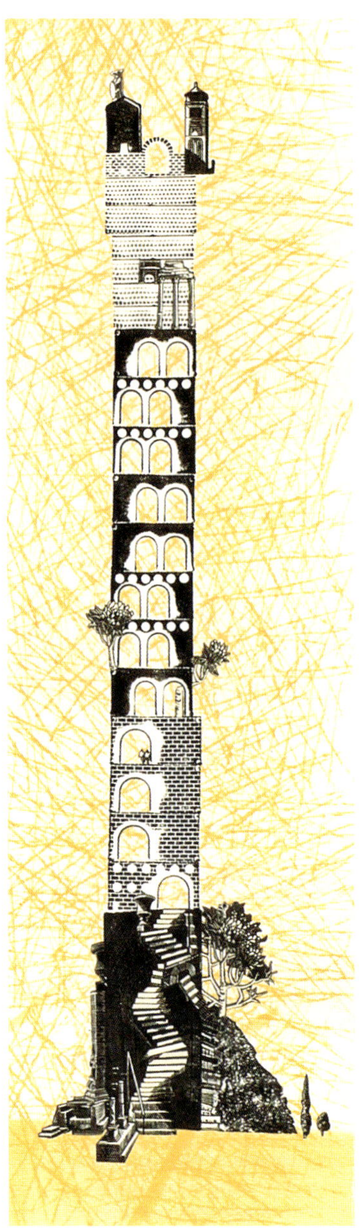

200. Desert Tower

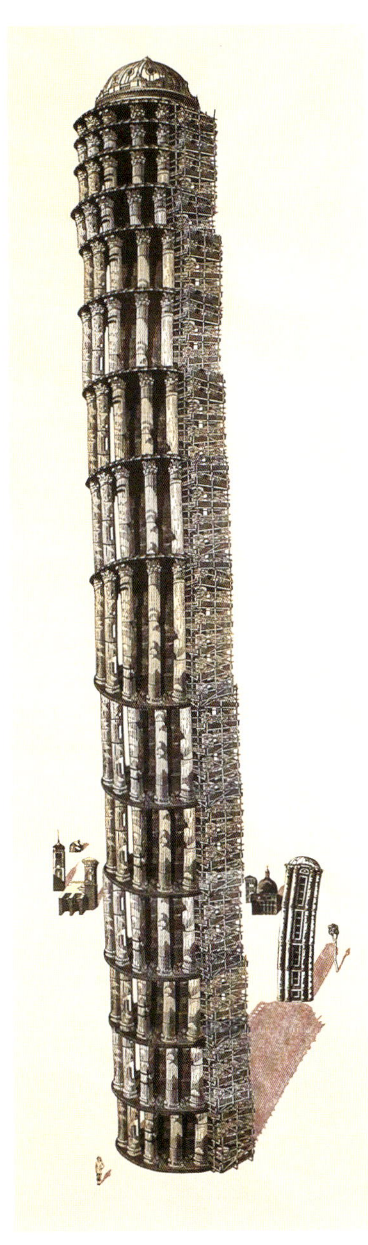

176. Self-portrait with Towers

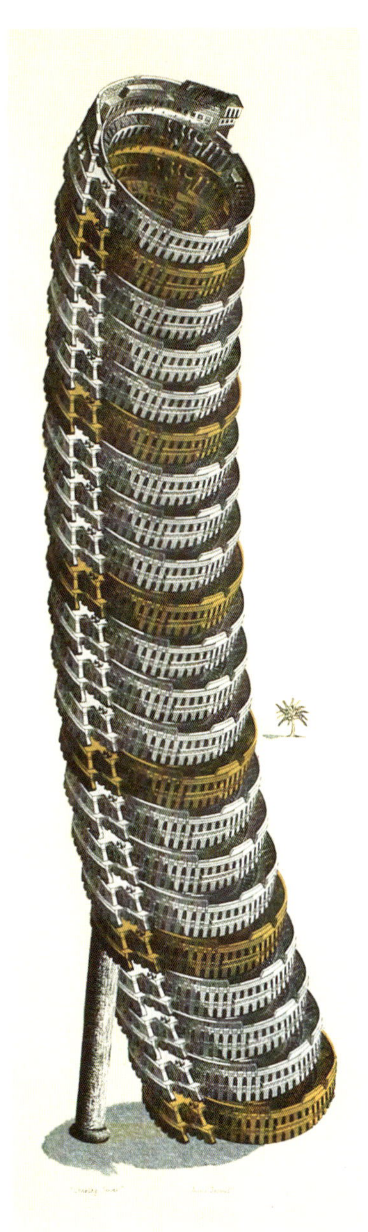

112. Leaning Tower

179 **Taormina**

1995   95 x 55 mm   Edition: 3   Linocut

A reduction linocut in three colours which was made to test the printing of lino with water-based ink, prior to conducting a print workshop in linocutting – using water-based inks – for *Paintworks Ltd.*

180 **Study (after Dürer)**

1995   100 x 75 mm   Edition: 12 A/P's   Woodcut

British Museum (Education Department) & private collections

Commissioned by the British Museum Education Service for video demonstrating Dürer's printmaking techniques, it is a study of the head of Hercules from Dürer's *Hercules & the Molionide Twins.*

181 * **Panorama**

(p. 60)   1995   128 x 372 mm   Edition: 40   Wood engraving

Prizewinner – RWA Open Print Exhibition, Bristol 1997

Ashmolean Museum, Ex Libris Museum (Moscow, Russia) & private collections

A wood engraving, the components of which I engraved on several blocks of varying shapes and sizes which were then reassembled like a jigsaw puzzle and printed. The image is based on a pencil and grey wash drawing I made from a hill above the town of S. Severino, in the Marches region of Italy, in 1994. The final print, like no. 118, is intended to suggest ancient fragments of fresco as well as reflecting an interest in the abstract, irregular shapes created by the printed blocks.

182 **Building Bridges on Thin Ice**

1996   170 x 380 mm   Edition: 1   Wood engraving, coloured

Private collection   Japanese papers & collage

An invented composition suggested by the Accademia bridge in Venice. The bridge and buildings were constructed largely from repeated details of nos. 74, 118, 120 and 159 while the reflections in the river and colours in the ice were made of torn pieces of a green proof of no. 80, collaged with *Amaretti* wrappers and assembled like no. 126.

183 **London Terraces**

1996   140 x 451 mm   Edition: 1   Wood engraving & collage

A composition of repeated elements from state proofs of no. 195 collaged onto a sheet of Japanese Gampi Vellum to create a sweeping terrace of houses.

184 **View from Above**

1996   76 x 95 mm   Edition: 1   Wood engraving, linocut,

Private collection   gold leaf & collage

The diptych format for this work (and for no. 187) was produced by inking and printing the then uncut, roughly sanded engraving blocks which were later to become the matrices for no. 198. Onto this background, I collaged an imaginary aerial view using details of nos. 118 and 181, with areas of colour provided by red/brown and green fragments of nos. 80 and 81.

185 **Church by Night**

1996   76 x 126 mm   Edition: 1   Wood engraving, linocut, marbling,

black crayon & collage

The triptych format for this work was produced as for no. 184 with another rectangular, roughly sanded, uncut block printed in the middle. Onto this background, I collaged three views of the exterior and interior of an imaginary church (using elements from nos. 74, 80, 138, and 178). The composition, especially the central section, was suggested by the curved patterns in the printing of the roughly sanded boxwood.

186 * Isola Tiberina

(p. 37)   1996   420 x 330 mm   Edition: 1   Wood engraving, linocut, screenprint,
                                                                                                 pencil, watercolour, marbling,
                                                                                                 coloured papers, gold leaf & collage

This composition was suggested by a postcard of an aerial view of Rome's Tiber Island and a pencil and wash drawing (made in 1994). It is constructed primarily from details of nos. 74, 103, 120, 159, 181 and (green proofs of) 80. The trees were created in a similar manner to those in no. 130 and the mottled colour of the water was provided by a large piece of an unsuccessful screenprint which I started but never completed in about 1986.

187   Homage to Giotto

         1996   76 x 90 mm   Edition: 1   Wood engraving, gold leaf & collage
                      Private collection

Onto the diptych background I collaged an imaginary view of miscellaneous architectural fragments from nos. 74, 138, 159, 178 and 194. The image was designed to recall the architecture portrayed in Giotto's extraordinary fresco cycle of the life of St Francis, at Assisi. Since the recent tragic earthquake devastation of these frescoes, this little collage has taken on a particular poignancy for me.

188   The Pile of Bricks

         1996   80 x 330 x 13 mm   Edition: 1   Wood engraving, archival
                                                                                                 paper tape & collage

A further development of the theme and format of no. 127. However, whereas in no. 127, the townscape collapses in on itself, in this collage, the town develops, brick by brick, but seems unstable, like a child's brick tower which could be toppled at any moment. The collage is made of tiny details from nos. 75 and 159. The title is an intentional reference to the Tate Gallery's notorious exhibit.

189 * Building the Viale Foro Imperiale

(p. 40)   1996   120 x 305 x 6 mm   Edition: 1   Wood engraving, linocut &
                                                                                                 collage on gessoed panel

This was the first of a series of works where the paper elements of the collage are adhered to painted, gessoed, wood panels. It is composed, primarily, from torn, cut and reassembled colour versions of no. 102, as well as details of nos. 74, 103, 118, 120 and 121. The idea pursues an ongoing interest in creating a contemporary image but one which hopefully evokes the timeless flavour of ancient fresco and also perhaps provokes reflection on the "progress" of man's perpetual need to rebuild and reinvent his cities. The subject-matter refers to Mussolini's construction of the vast Viale Foro Imperiale which cuts a swathe through Rome's most ancient archaeological sites between the Victor Emmanuel II monument and the Colosseum. This road-building project necessitated the demolition of many medieval churches and apartments which, in their turn, were built over parts of the ancient Roman forum.

190   Moscow

         1996   108 x 60 x 6 mm   Edition: 1   Wood engraving, collage & gold leaf
                      Private collection   on gessoed panel

A view of the Kremlin and some Stalinist-style architecture collaged from details of a Russian banknote and proofs of nos. 74, 118 and 120. It reflects an impression of the city gained during a visit there, in 1995, when I had a solo exhibition at the Ex Libris Museum.

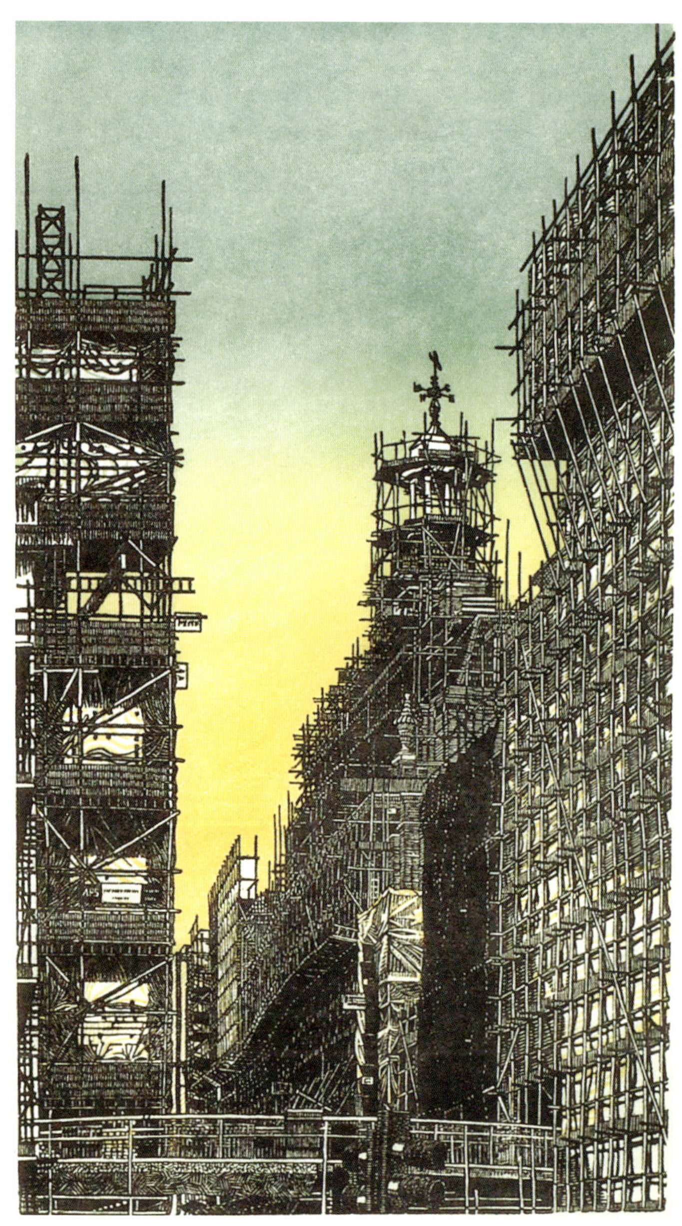

199. Bishopsgate, London, in the 1990s

191   Fragile Institutions

 1996   203 x 127 x 6 mm   Edition: 1   Wood engraving, collage & gold leaf
                                                                                      on gessoed panel

A work with a comparable theme and structure to no. 189. The towers are made of repeated details from nos. 118 and 120. It reflects the custom, in medieval Italy, for wealthy families to build towers of ever-increasing height – as symbols of status and prosperity (much the same motives as may have led to the construction of contemporary British developments such as London's Canary Wharf tower). These ancient structures were not always built upon adequate foundations and their stability was further undermined by a continuing regional problem with earth tremors and by the fact that the owners had a tendency to add additional storeys to already-constructed towers each time their wealth increased, or in order to surpass the height of a neighbouring rival's building. Such additions (as can still be witnessed today in Italy's towns and cities such as S. Gimignano and Bergamo) often rendered the original edifices unstable on their pre-existing foundations and led to their collapse like a child's over-ambitious construction of toy bricks.

192   Castel S. Angelo

 1996   197 x 222 x 6 mm   Edition: 1   Wood engraving, linocut, marbling
                                                                                      & pencil on gessoed panel

An aerial view of Rome's Castel S. Angelo, loosely based on a postcard and memories of the building itself. The castle is composed of elements of nos. 74, 102, 103, 138, 178 and 181 combined with pencil drawing – and marbled paper (which I made in 1987/8 at an evening class in book-binding at the London College of Printing).

193   Marble Tower

 1996   197 x 114 x 6 mm   Edition: 1   Linocut, wood engraving, marbling,
               Private collection   pencil & collage on gessoed panel

A variation on the theme of no. 191. The tower comprises a repeated detail from no. 103, collaged onto a background of marbled paper on painted, gessoed panel. The other buildings primarily comprise pieces of a Russian banknote and a detail of no. 162.

194   London Gardens

 1996   125 x 55 mm   Edition: 30   Wood engraving
               Private collections

Commissioned for a portfolio project entitled *Gardens in Relief,* this is an early morning view from the top floor of my home, looking out over the back garden to the houses in the next road. This image evolved from a combination of photographs and sketches of the light and shade at about 8.30 a.m.

195   London Gardens (2nd state)

 1996   125 x 55 mm   Edition: 40   Wood engraving
               Private collections

A development of no. 194 with further engraving on the same block to make the whole image lighter and with stronger contrasts of sun and shade – reflecting the light later in the morning, at about 10.30 a.m.

196 * Kremlin Christmas

(p. 53)   1996   190 x 145 mm   Edition: 1   Wood engraving, pencil & collage

A collage comprising details of nos. 74, 120, 159 and 178 combined with fragments of Russian banknotes to create an impression of the Kremlin, visited during my trip to Russia in 1995. The truck carrying away a demolished church spire along with a toppled monument to an anonymous hero of the State reflected thoughts about Russia's ongoing state of flux where, in former times, physical embodiments of religious observance were demolished to make way for Stalinist symbols of power. Now, however, many of these secular monuments are being removed and the Church's influence is in the ascendant.

197   Slate Hill

    1996   120 x 220 mm   Edition: Slate rubbing with collaged wood engraving

An invented Italianate hill town whose title reflects the fact that its basic shape is made from an inked, printed piece of roofing slate (onto which I collaged details of nos. 118, 139, 159, 162 and 181).

198   Architectural Salvage, Hoxton

    1996   76 x 95 mm   Edition: 40   Wood engraving
                   Private collections

An engraving combining a disparate collection of salvaged religious and secular artefacts, seen in a yard in east London. They are engraved as a diptych, suggesting religious significance, to imply the value (both commercial and spiritual) often placed on these material items by one section of society – having been discarded for scrap by another.

199 *   Bishopsgate, London, in the 1990s

(p. 48)   1996   330 x 184 mm   Edition: 40   Linocut
                   Ashmolean Museum & private collections

This view of London's banking district, shrouded in scaffolding, was developed from studies and photographs after a bomb devastated the area. The little scaffolded turret reminded me of Japanese pagodas; and the blended background colours were selected to reflect the characteristic amber and turquoise hues of sun and sky which appear in Japanese prints. As I find it hard to think of Japan without images of the bomb at Hiroshima coming to mind, these colours also seemed appropriate to hint at the menace of unlooked-for destruction – even in a comparatively minor explosion such as this.

200 *   Desert Tower

(p. 44)   1996   425 x 124 mm   Edition: 1   Mixed media monoprint with wood engraved collage

The pedestal is a print from the uncut block which also comprises the central section of no. 185. The jagged rocky buttress is a piece of printed roofing slate. The main structure of the tower is a series of repeated printings of different facets of a child's toy (a free gift in a chocolate egg) – a tiny plastic house with arched doorways, brick-effect walls and a slate-like pattern on the roof. The textured amber background was made by a roller, with string wrapped around the rubber, which was inked and rolled directly onto the collage. (The printed tower was masked out with a paper stencil before adding this colour.) The image was completed by the collaged additions of fragments of nos. 74, 138, 159, 162 and 198. This work develops ideas pursued in various other collages such as nos. 188, 191 and 193. The particular mixed media construction of this and no. 197 arose from printed experiments I was making for a book of relief printing techniques.

201   Landmarks

    1996   510 x 420 mm   Edition: 1   Linocut, pencil & collage

These towers are composed, largely, of details of colour trial proofs of no. 202.

202   Excavations, Afternoon

    1996   610 x 203 mm   Edition: 40   Linocut

A view from the Capitol hill looking over part of the Roman forum, past the remains of the Temple of Vespasian, to the Arch of Septimius Severus and the church of Santi Luca e Martina beyond. The image was developed from a pencil and grey wash drawing made late one afternoon in June 1994.

203   Cement Mixer

    1996   22 x 22 mm   Edition: 1   Wood engraving, gold leaf, Indian coloured paper & collage

A miniature variation on the structure and theme of no. 175. The image is a non-specific London scene of tower blocks, churches and building sites and comprises fragments of nos. 178 and 195.

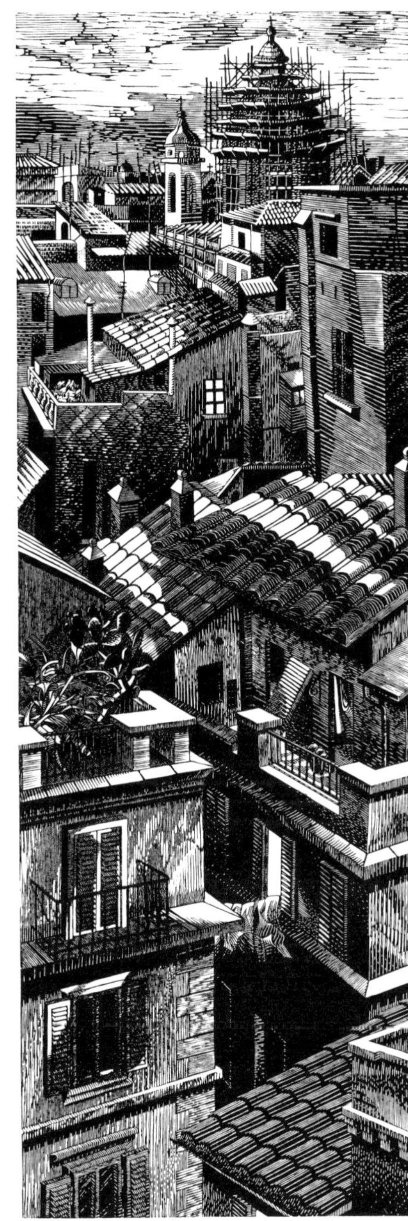

123. Roma

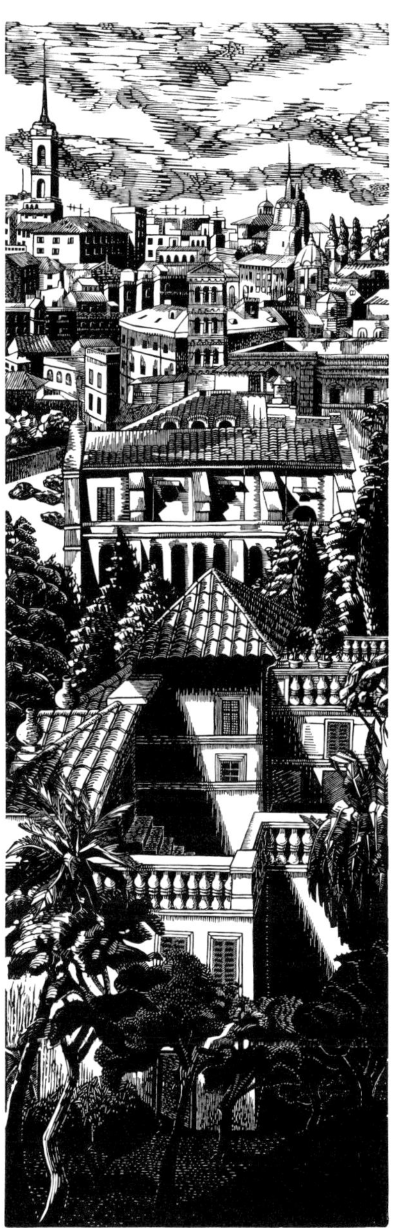

134. Roma dal Aventino

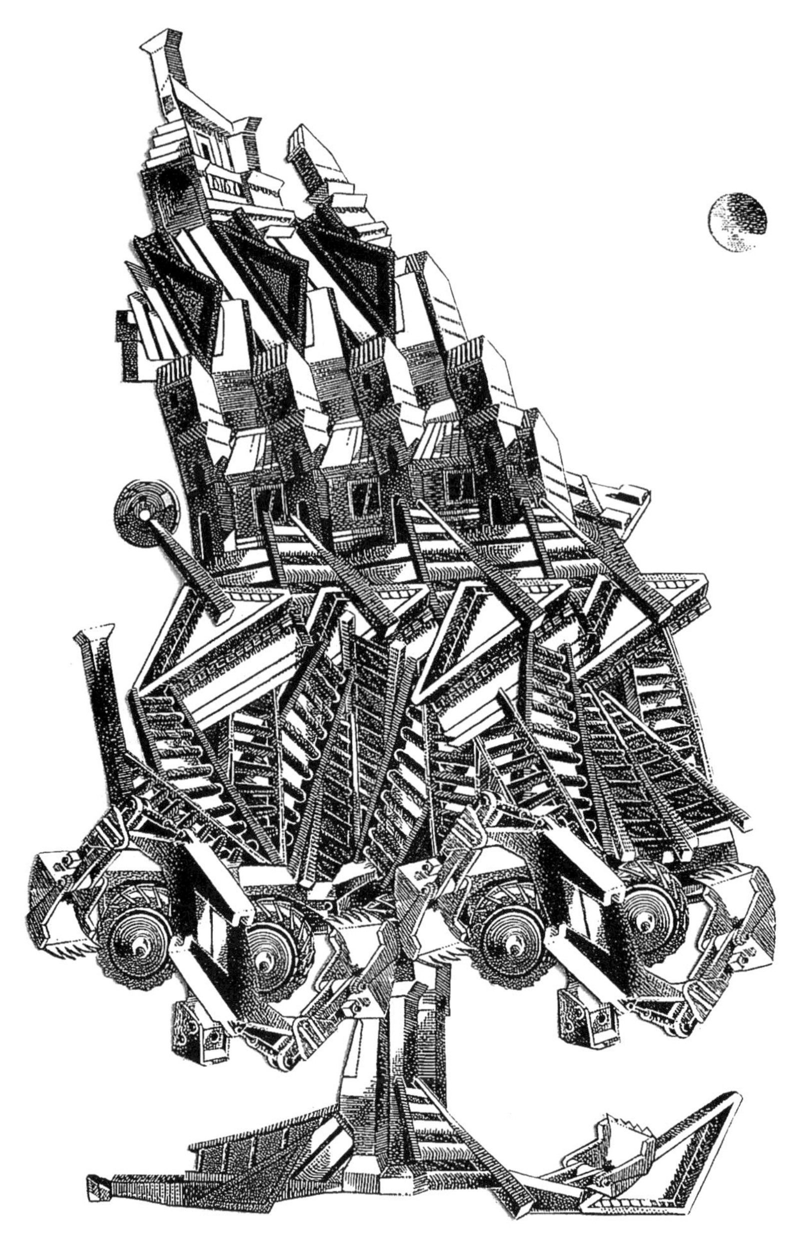

133. 21st Century Christmas Tree

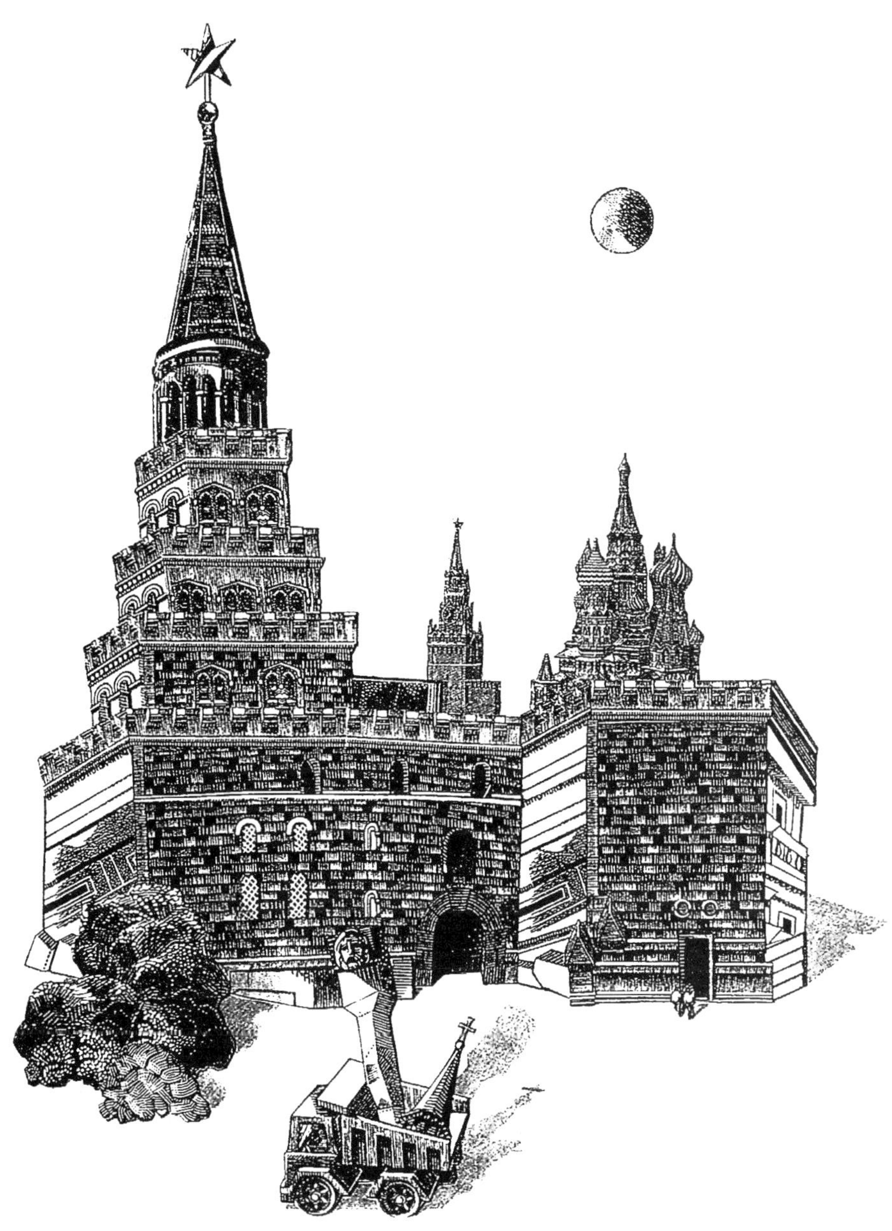

196. Kremlin Christmas

204 Sotheby's, New Bond Street

1996	93 x 70 mm	Not editioned	Wood engraving

Sotheby's & private collections

Commissioned by Sotheby's Auctioneers.

205 * London Gardens – diptych

(p. 56) 1997   125 x 120 mm   Edition: 75   Wood engraving

Prizewinner – Art Review Award, The National Print Exhibition, London 1998
Art Review & private collections

A wood engraving in two parts which depicts one scene: that of my irregularly-shaped back garden with its zigzag slash of boundary wall picked out in the early morning sun which slants diagonally across the terrace of houses beyond. I look out at this particular view every day, from the top floor of my home in Hackney, east London. The complete image evolved in two stages, each of which I engraved on separate endgrain blocks of box wood, with an interval of about a year between the completion of the left "panel" of the diptych (editioned in its own right as no. 195) and the commencement of the right.

206 Bath Circus I

1997   120 x 130 mm   Edition: 40   Wood engraving

Private collections

An image based on a postcard view and pencil studies of Bath Circus. As in nos. 36, 102 and 136, the image was suggested by (and designed to fill) the circular shape of the block. I editioned at this stage of cutting to create a first stage of an evolving series of versions of this print; and secondly to create a more starkly black and white, less tonally detailed engraving than usual – reflecting an interest in the minimally cut but powerful engravings by Edward Wadsworth.

207 * Bath Circus II

(p. 57) 1997   120 x 130 mm   Edition: 75   Wood engraving

Private collections

A development of no. 206 with further engraving on the same block to make the whole image lighter, with greater areas of detail, tone and texture. I am working on a third version of this image which will introduce areas of colour.

208 Knot Garden

1997   46 x 42 mm   Edition: 50   Wood engraving

Private collections

Commissioned by Mrs M Paice, Bourton House, Bourton-on-the-Hill, near Moreton in Marsh, Gloucestershire.

209 Bankside Power Station

1997   360 x 125 mm   Edition: 1   Monotype

A monotype drawing developed from one of a number of pencil, wash and watercolour sketches made of London's Bankside Power Station in early 1995, just before building work began to commence its reincarnation as a new Tate Gallery.

210 I Sassi, Matera

1997   285 x 203 mm   Edition: 1   Monotype

A monotype drawing developed from one of a series of pencil and grey wash drawings made, in autumn 1996, of the ancient southern Italian hill town of Matera, most of whose buildings are carved out of the rockface of the hill – an extraordinary transmutation which gives the whole haphazard warren of stepped streets and dwellings an organic aspect.

211 Roman Rooftop View

1997   285 x 195 mm   Edition: 1   Monotype

A monotype drawing developed from a pencil (and very light wash) study, made in 1992, looking over Roman rooftops towards the Church of S. Andrea della Valle.

212   Teatro Greco, Taormina
      1997   145 x 100 mm   Edition: 1   Monotype
A monotype drawing of the Teatro Greco at Taormina, Sicily, developed from a number of pencil, wash and watercolour drawings made there in 1992.

213   Syracuse by Night
      1997   170 x 125 mm   Edition: 1   Monotype
A monotype developed from a nighttime sketch (made in 1992, in pencil and grey wash) of the ruined Palazzo Montalto in Syracuse, Sicily.

214   Umbrian Landscape
      1997   305 x 180 mm   Edition: 12   Indented plywood print
I made this print, in an unfamiliar technique, as an experiment (like nos. 197 and 200) for a book (commissioned by A & C Black publishers Ltd) of relief print processes. It is a view seen from the Umbrian hill town of Todi and is a development of a pencil drawing made there in 1995.

215   Umbrian Landscape II
      1997   259 x 180 mm   Edition: 1   Monotype
A development of no. 214 using the same drawing as its basis.

216   Cingoli in the Rain
      1997   221 x 150 mm   Edition: 1   Monotype
A monotype developed from a swift, grey wash sketch (made in 1994, in a twenty minute interval between torrential rain showers) of a view from the hilltown of Cingoli, in the Marches region of Italy.

217   The British Library
      1998   144 x 126 mm   Special edition: 75   Wood engraving
                    British Library collection   Second edition: 25
Commissioned by the British Library for a permanent exhibition explaining print processes.

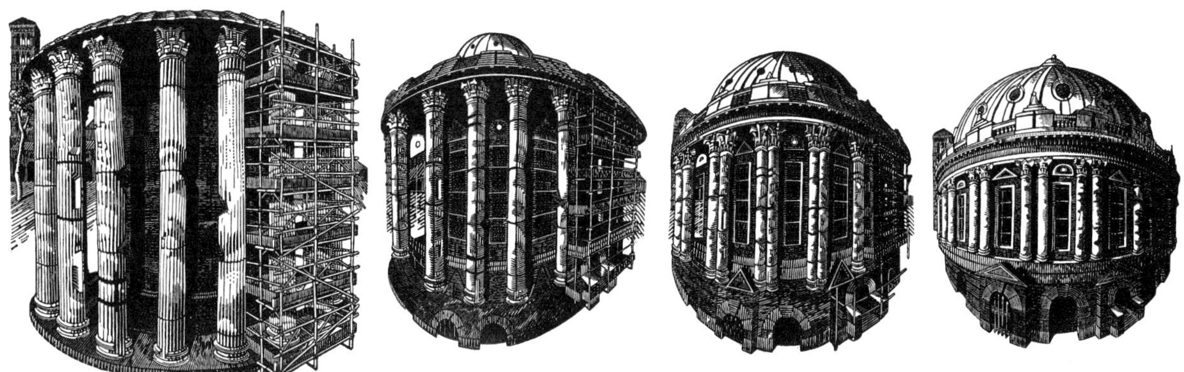

138. Rotunda x 4

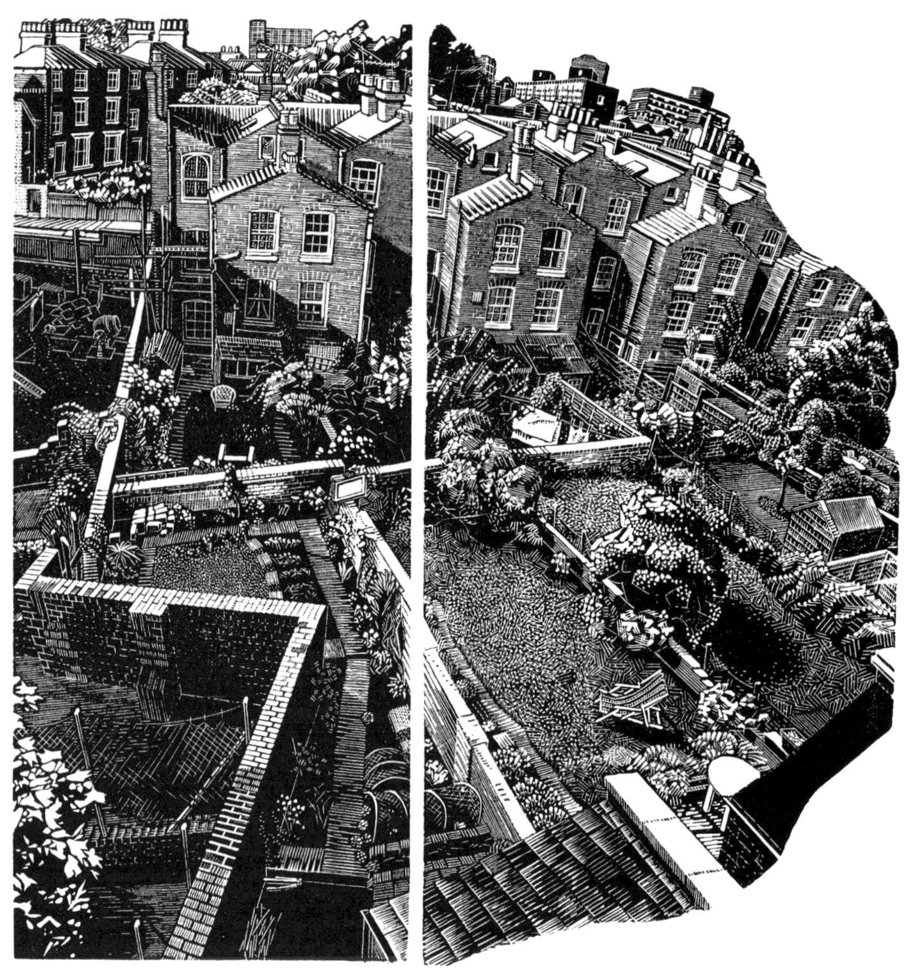

205. London Gardens – diptych

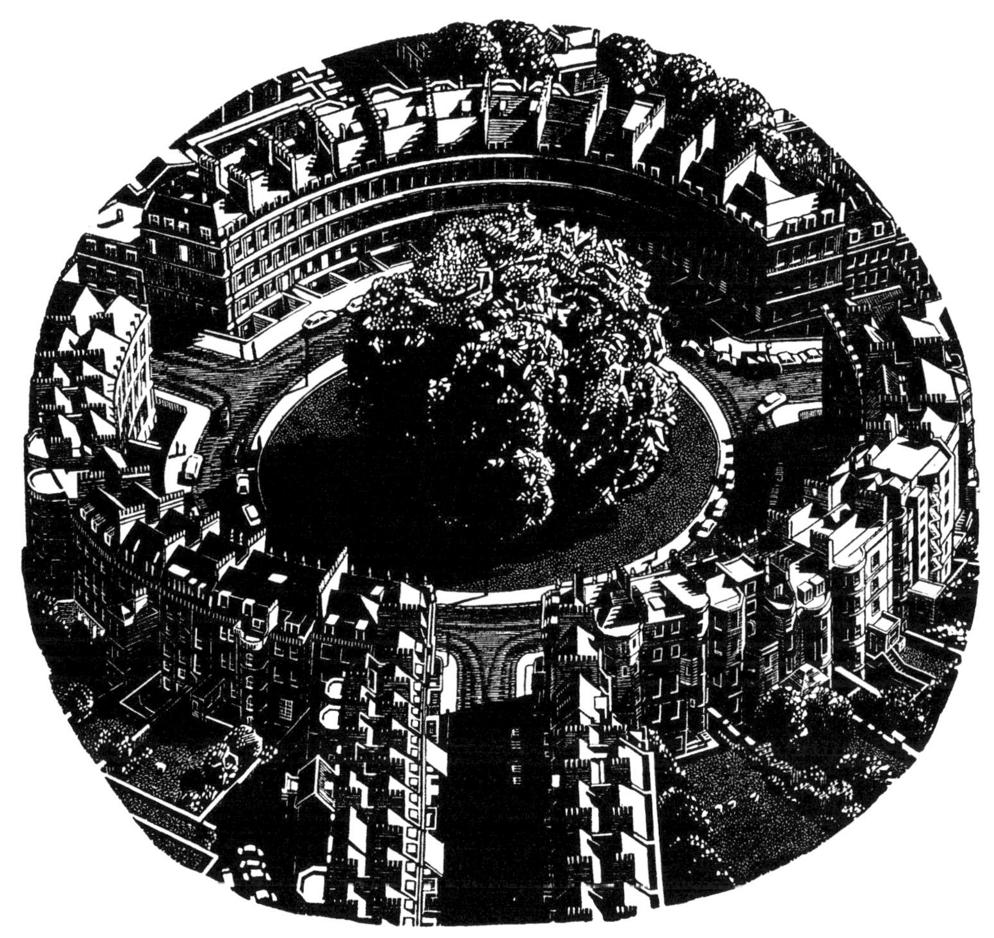

207. *Bath Circus II*

Anne Desmet

14/6/64	Born in Liverpool, England (youngest of three children)
1964 – 70	Lived with family in father's hotel, Toxteth, Liverpool
1970 – 71	A year spent in hospital (the longest of many lengthy periods between 1966 & 1985, undergoing surgery to correct congenital hip dislocation)
1972	Moved with family to private house, Hightown, Liverpool
14/7/73	Death of father, Louis Desmet
1975 – 83	Secondary School education: Seafield Grammar School (1975 – 77) which became Sacred Heart High School, Crosby, Liverpool
1983 – 86	BA Fine Art, Ruskin School of Drawing & Fine Art/ Worcester College, Oxford University
1987 – 88	Advanced Studies in Printmaking Postgraduate Diploma, Central School of Art & Design, London
1989 – 90	Lived & worked in Rome, Italy
1991	MA Fine Art, Oxford University
1993	Bought current home/studio in Hackney, London
2/6/94	Married Roy Willingham
25/9/97	Birth of son, Thomas Louis Albert

Awards & prizes

1987	Lithography Prize, Printmakers Council (PMC) & Whatman Paper *National Print Exhibition*, Royal Festival Hall, London
1988	Elected Associate of the Royal Society of Painter-Printmakers (RE)
1989 & 96	The Elizabeth Greenshields Foundation (Montreal, Canada) award for representational/ figurative work in Printmaking
1989 – 90	British School at Rome Scholarship in Printmaking
1990	Artist-in-Residence, Oriel 31 (Davies Memorial Gallery), Newtown, Powys
1991	Rooks Rider Prize, *A View of the New Exhibition*, Royal Over-seas League, London Elected Fellow of the RE Elected Member of the Society of Wood Engravers (SWE)
1992	Prizewinner, *South Bank Picture Show*, Royal Festival Hall, London
1994	The Gordon Tuffrey Memorial Award, *Royal West of England Academy (RWA) Open Print Exhibition*
1995	Exhibition Medal – Ex Libris Museum, Moscow
1997	The S Dawson Taylor Award for a wood engraving, *RWA Open Print Exhibition*
1998	The *Art Review* Award, *National Print Exhibition*, Mall Galleries, London

Solo exhibitions

1990	Ruskin School of Drawing & Fine Art, Oxford
1991, 92, 94, 96 & 98	Duncan Campbell Contemporary Art, London
1992	Royal Overseas League, London
1993 & 95	Godfrey & Twatt Gallery, Harrogate
1995	Ex Libris Museum, Moscow, Russia
1998	*Towers & Transformations:* a retrospective exhibition, Ashmolean Museum, Oxford (& touring UK, 1999)

Two/three person exhibitions

1984	Worcester College, Oxford
1985	St John's College, Oxford
1987	Old Fire Station Arts Centre, Oxford
1993	Barbican Centre, London
1996	Printworks Gallery, Colchester

Selected art writing, lecturing & related experience

1989	Visiting lecturer in Fine Art/Printmaking, Leeds Polytechnic
1990 – 91	Lecturer in Fine Art/Printmaking, Royal Academy Schools, London
1990 – 94	Visiting lecturer in Fine Art/Printmaking, Ruskin School of Art, Oxford
1991	Part-time administrator, Hardware Gallery, London
1991 – 97	Member of selection committee for 9 national & international open print exhibitions
1991 –	Visiting lecturer in Fine Art/Printmaking, Middlesex University (ongoing appointment)
1992 – 95	Honorary Curator of prints, RE Council
1993 – 95	Free-lance art reporter for the *Church Times*
1993 – 97	Print Manager, Bankside Gallery, London (gallery administrator, 1988 – 93) Editor of *Bankside Bulletin*, the quarterly journal of the RWS & the RE
1995 – 97	Honorary Secretary, RE Council
1996	Visiting lecturer in Fine Art/business studies, College of North East London
1996 – 98	Co-author, for A & C Black publishers Ltd, of book of printmaking techniques
1998	Visiting lecturer in wood engraving, Royal Academy Schools, London
1998 –	Appointed as editor of *Printmaking Today*, a quarterly journal of contemporary, international graphic art

Selected commissions

1987   Wood engraving of & for Central School of Art &
Design, London
1988   Wood engraved illustrations for *Young Dragon Book
of Verse* published by Oxford University Press
1991 – 93 23 wood engraved illustrations for *The Times*
1995   Wood engraving, in an edition of 250, of & for
Balliol College, Oxford
Watercolour of the Queen Elizabeth Hospital for
Children, east London
Woodcut of enlarged detail of head of Hercules
(from *Hercules & the Molionide Twins* by Dürer); &
filmed demonstration of woodcutting techniques for
British Museum/National Gallery video
1996   Wood engraved logo for Sotheby's Auctioneers
of their New Bond Street, London, premises
1998   Wood engraving of gateway & forecourt of the new
British Library, London: print & engraved block form
part of a permanent exhibition of print processes at
the Library

Selected group exhibitions

1987   *PMC & Whatman Paper National Print Exhibition*,
Royal Festival Hall, London
1988   *Manchester Academy of Fine Arts 129th Exhibition*
Bankside Gallery Open Print Exhibition, London
8 times since 1988
The SWE Annual Exhibition (touring UK)
1989   *The US – UK Print Connection*,
Barbican Centre, London (& touring UK)
1990   *Mostra 1990*, British School at Rome, Italy
Rome Scholars 1980 – 1990,
Royal College of Art, London
International Open Exhibition of Miniature Prints,
Intaglio Printmaker Gallery, London
11th British International Print Biennale,
Cartwright Hall, Bradford (& touring UK)
7 times since 1990
Royal Academy of Arts Summer Exhibition, London
1991   *PMC/British High Commission Exhibition*, Valetta &
International Malta Festival, Malta
Contemporary British Prints, Scarborough Art Gallery
Print Europe, Barbican Centre, London (& touring)
1991, 93 & 97
Royal Over-Seas League Annual Open Exhibition,
London
1991, 95 & 98
The Discerning Eye, Mall Galleries, London

1991, 94 & 97
RWA Open Print Exhibition, Bristol
Annually since 1991
The RE Annual Members' Exhibition,
Bankside Gallery, London
1992   *Contemporary Avant-Garde British Printmaking*,
Plymouth City Art Gallery
Images of Italy, Susan Duval Gallery, Colorado, USA
1992 & 97 *Salon des Graphiques*, Curwen Gallery, London
1993   *Bradford Open Print Exhibition*,
Cartwright Hall, Bradford
Adam & Co/The Spectator Art Award,
Edinburgh & Christies, London
1993, & 97 *Xylon International Print Triennale*,
Gewerbemuseum, Winterthur, Switzerland
(& touring worldwide)
1994   *Triennale Mondiale d'Estampes Petit Format*,
Chamalières, France (& touring Europe)
1994 & 97 *British International Miniature Print Exhibition*
(touring UK)
1994, 95 & 97
PMC National Open Print Exhibition, UK
Annually since 1994
National Print Exhibition, Mall Galleries, London
The Contemporary Print Show, Barbican Centre,
London
1995   *PMC 30th Anniversary Exhibition*,
Durham Light Infantry Museum
Best of Britain, House of Commons,
Westminster, London
*International Buchmesse der Kleinverlage und
Handpressen*, Mainzer, Germany
Fusion (an exhibition of innovative printmaking),
Hardware Gallery, London
1995/6   *Wood Engraving Here & Now*, SWE 75th Anniversary
Exhibition, Ashmolean Museum (& touring UK)
Building Blocks, Ikon Gallery, Birmingham –
touring exhibition
1996   *Europese Biennale voor Grafische Kunsten*,
Stadshallen Markt, Brugge, Belgium
1997   *International Miniature Print Competition 1997*,
Connecticut Graphic Arts Center, Norwalk CT, USA
1998   *The Royal Society of Painter-Printmakers*,
National Arts Club, New York &
Connecticut Graphic Arts Center, USA
Built, an exhibition by *The Artists' Network*, London
*Grafinnova '98, The 7th Open International
Triennial of Prints & Drawings*,
Ostrobothnian Museum, Vaasa, Finland

Collections

Ashmolean Museum; Victoria & Albert Museum;
National Art Library; British Museum (Education
Service); British Library; Fitzwilliam Museum,
Cambridge; Ex Libris Museum, Moscow, Russia;
Musée d'Art Contemporain, Chamalières, France;
Worcester College, Oxford; Balliol College, Oxford;
Manchester University; the National Grid plc;
IMG Corporate, New York, USA; *Art Review*;
& private collections worldwide

Selected bibliography

Spring 91   *Watercolours, Drawings & Prints* (Vol 6, No 1) –
             "Ideas for Images" by Anne Desmet
1992   *Engravers Two* – a handbook compiled for the SWE
             (published by Silent Books)
Jan 1993   *Art Review – Roma* (linocut) – prizewinner at
             South Bank Picture Show

Summer 93   *Printmaking Today* (Vol 2, No 2) – "Anne Desmet:
             Collaged Wood Engravings" by Rosemary Simmons
4/12/93   *The Times* – "Against the Grain of Fashion –
             Modern Wood Engravers" by Jim McCue
Jan 1994   *Burlington Magazine* – "Acquisitions at the
             Ashmolean Museum" by Timothy Wilson
1994   *Wood Engraving and the Woodcut in Britain
             c1890 – 1990* by James Hamilton
             (published by Barrie & Jenkins)
Nov 1994   *Art Monthly* – "Amazing Grace" – artists' books
             recommended by Cathy Courtney
Feb 1995   *Art Review* – "Art under £1,000" –
             recommendations by Nicola Shane
9/1/96   *Woman's Hour (Radio 4)* – interview by Sylvia Horn
Sep 1997   *Art Review* (Print Supplement) – feature
May 1998   *Art Review* – "An Artist's Eye" –
             feature by Anne Desmet

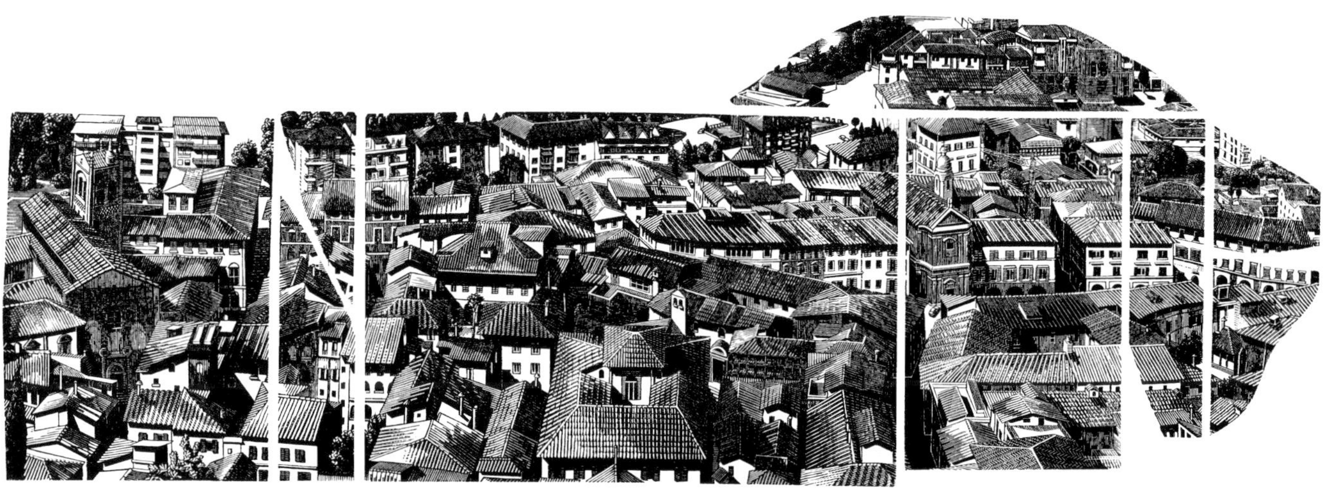

181. Panorama